ARE AMERICANS REALLY THIS STUPID?

ARE POLITICIANS REALLY THIS INEPT?

SCOTT F. PARADIS

https://ScottFParadis.com

Books by **Scott F. Paradis:**

ARE AMERICANS REALLY THIS STUPID?
Are Politicians Really This Inept?

CAPITOL CRIMES
Is That a Knife in Your Back?

SHEEP, HERDERS, WOLVES
Why We Are Where We Are: A Modern American Fable

EXPLOSIVE LEADERSHIP
The Ultimate Leader Training Experience

MONEY
The New Science of Making It

HIGH PERFORMANCE HEALTH AND FITNESS HABITS
Engage Your Health and Fitness Auto-Pilot

HIGH PERFORMANCE HABITS
Making Success a Habit

HOW TO SUCCEED AT ANYTHING
In 3 Simple Steps

SUCCESS 101 HOW LIFE WORKS
Know the Rules, Play to Win

WARRIORS DIPLOMATS HEROES
Why America's Army Succeeds
Lessons for Business and Life

PROMISE AND POTENTIAL
A Life of Wisdom, Courage, Strength, and Will

And coming soon:

FOLLOW THE MONEY
It's Never About the Money

BUILD ME A SON
Courage and Hope Forge a Man

COMPETE OR CREATE
Your Choice

POWER
Why So Few Have So Much While So Many Have So Little

BE
A Messenger of Hope,
An Example of Faith and an Expression of Love

ARE YOU REALLY BETTER THAN AVERAGE?
Where You Really Stand and the Fastest Way to the Top

NOTHING OUT OF THE ORDINARY
EVERYTHING'S EXTRAORDINARY
Life's as Great as You THINK

Life changing online courses and workshops by

Scott F. Paradis

https://ScottFParadis.com

FOLLOW THE MONEY

It's Never About the Money

EXPLOSIVE LEADERSHIP

The Ultimate Leader Training Experience

HIGH PERFORMANCE HEALTH AND FITNESS HABITS

Engage Your Health and Fitness Auto-Pilot

SUCCESS 101 HOW LIFE WORKS

Focus on Fundamentals

Looking for a motivating presenter?

Scott F. Paradis Keynote Themes

FOLLOW THE MONEY
It's Never About the Money

SHEEP HERDERS WOLVES
The Time for You to Lead is NOW

Nothing Out of the Ordinary
Everything's Extraordinary
It's as Great as You THINK

https://ScottFParadis.com

ARE AMERICANS REALLY THIS STUPID?
ARE POLITICIANS REALLY THIS INEPT?

Published and distributed by:

Cornerstone Achievements
Alaska, Virginia, New Hampshire USA
www.cornerstone-achievements.com

ISBN: 978-0-9863821-8-5 (digital)

ISBN: 978-0-9863821-9-2 (print, soft cover)

Published in the United States of America.

This book is dedicated to

Men and women who seek the truth,
THINK
and then act for the greater good.

CONTENTS

The most consequential of all decisions:

Choosing to embrace either

FEAR, LACK and LIMIT

or

LOVE, ABUNDANCE and OPPORTUNITY

One option is to compete, the other to collaborate.

This single decision determines the course of one's life and the destiny of one's society.

PROLOGUE

America was seen for a time as a beacon on a hill. A mythological place where anything was possible. Armed with a dream and willing to put forth the effort, people could make something of themselves. While America never realized its full potential, in an often violent and sometimes unforgiving world America offered hope. It still offers hope, but the beacon is fading.

Hope opens the door to opportunity and opportunity leads to prosperity when people are willing to do what needs to be done together. Americans, relying on the promise and potential of liberty maintained by the rule of law, strived to improve, sought to achieve, and made the most of themselves. Americans brought a magnificent dream to life. And yet, we have nearly squandered it all.

The answer to my deliberately provocative question: "***Are Americans really this stupid?***" is yes **and** no.

Consider the oft-cited definition of insanity: *'Doing the same thing over and over again and expecting a different result.'* While we aspire to opportunity and prosperity by means of self-governance, we Americans keep screwing up. We keep making the same mistakes again and again. When will we learn? Can we learn?

It is not that Americans are stupid in that we do not have the capacity or ability to make sense of reality, recognize a mutually beneficial path, and do the right thing. Rather, we lack the will to see clearly, reason, and act collectively for a more significant benefit. We instead see an opportunity for personal advantage now, a chance to get ours, the prospect to win, to beat others out, and in the moment, we seize it. Good for now. Not so good for what comes next.

We deliberately choose an *every-man-for-himself*, *survival-of-the-fittest* path and mistakenly expect that path will lead to prosperity. *Every man for himself* always results in pain and suffering. This is the way things are. But is it the way things must be?

Something else is afoot, something bigger than us as individuals. We are in the chaos and crisis phase of our natural 80-year social cycle, the creative-destruction phase. Individuals are being moved. Society is experiencing a plot twist. Caught unaware and off-guard, we did not see the plot twist coming. America is dying. This fading is the next step in the natural cycle. However, if we play our cards right, rather than destruction leading to generations of despair, we can usher in a rebirth to even more extraordinary achievement.

This crisis is an opportunity to change course and awaken from a self-destructive path.

In the social cycle's chaos and crisis phase, our natural human capacities for fear and greed and our natural tendency to conserve energy – our seemingly inexhaustible, sometimes obsessively compulsive attempt to get something for nothing –

express themselves most fervently. We collectively suffer under a cloud of delusion. It is as if most of us have drunk an elixir putting us under a spell. A self-serving, delusional, self-righteous virus has taken hold. Completely unable to see beyond our immediate selves, we suffer the "*zombie apocalypse*." People scramble about anxiously trying to find brains.

We did not get here overnight. The state of nature is to compete. Human beings have been competing violently for millennia. Somehow, however, we came to see an advantage in cooperating and collaborating rather than competing and killing, and civil society began. Yet civil society, like all things in nature, ebbs and flows in cycles.

A contemporary social cycle begins with people recognizing the advantage of cooperating, collaborating, and creating together. Over time, however, people find the conformity of community restrictive. Individuals begin to break out to discover and express themselves. Once on their own and gaining confidence, people instinctively compete against one another. Eventually, friendly competition devolves into *every-man-for-himself*, back to the fundamentals of nature, which always culminates in a crisis. The social cycle is as regular and predictable as seasons.

Chaos and crisis are creative destruction, the death of self-serving competition. The end can be slow, painful, and ultimately catastrophic or, if the people embrace the opportunity, can lead to a rebirth, a resurgence of community where the cycle begins again. It is a magnificent ride, except when immersed in the turmoil of chaos and crisis. Then, it seems like the end of the world.

The social cycle advances methodically and predictably. As people move from the "*pulling together*" phase of the social cycle into the awakening phase, some naturally compete better than others. Cunning competitors divide, misdirect, and play to others' fears and weaknesses. Over time, cunning and clever competitors concentrate political, social, and economic power in the hands of a few. The few live like kings, the many like peasants or, worse, slaves.

The powerless – the men and women who feel they have lost – get squeezed into a corner. In the chaos and crisis phase of the social cycle, people, sensing they have no attractive options, fall back to the seminal law of the jungle: *kill or be killed*; *us against the world*; *survival of the fittest*. Collectively the attitude becomes: Truth be damned. "Reality is what I say it is; whatever is good for me." As competition usurps civility, society's prospects dim.

Americans are not incapable of seeing the truth or seeing a better way. We are just willfully ignorant. Painfully, the social cycle exists to make us see the light. If you think I am employing hyperbole, consider the state of these United States.

POLITICAL MALPRACTICE

Fear, hate, violence, lies and deceit, a deadly pandemic; the United States Capitol ransacked by Americans; democracy under siege. Welcome to the United States in 2021.

As the year began, a new political administration rightly called for civility; unfortunately, civility, while a good start, is not enough. The unvarnished truth about the state of these United States is that we have dug ourselves a deep hole, and we are still digging.

All great empires come to an end. The American empire is no different. Most people, however, are surprised at how quickly this empire is collapsing. The American empire, while aided by unsympathetic competitive outside forces, is dying ultimately by way of suicide no less. This is the reality we face. This is where chaos and crisis dictate we be.

Is this really the end of America?

These are dark days in the United States of America, not brought on by an outside power or a foreign invader. No, we are experiencing rot from within, an assault on truth; fear and hate on a national scale. We are taking ourselves down. And we cannot seem to recognize this reality. That is the culmination phase of the social cycle manifesting in real-time.

Life advances through cycles, like seasons. Life blooms, grows, matures, declines, and dies. And so too, do societies. The United States of America is dying. But death is not the end. The United States can be born again. Americans, if we have the will, can find a way.

It is possible to advance boldly together, united in purpose to make the most of ourselves. But to progress, we must make some changes – we must ultimately change, end our fear-and-hate ways, and embrace enduring timeless principles. This need not be the end of America. It is up to Americans to decide.

Ultimately, this transition is not about changing the world out there. Trying to control people and circumstances got us into this mess in the first place. This transition, this transformation, is about fundamentally changing ourselves. When we change ourselves, our politics and our economics change as well. We can begin anew.

BIAS

Before I go on, you may be sifting for political party bias. So, I want to be clear. The foundation of our economic and social problems is not political. **Our problem is inherently and fundamentally spiritual.** If you are one of the many people who automatically reject any notion of spiritual redemption or spiritual alignment, I say to you – the spiritual is inherently and fundamentally practical. Spiritual is not other-dimensional, divorced from this reality or the pragmatic challenges of everyday life. The spiritual determines how we progress through the physical. Please bear with me.

The task at hand, the challenge ahead, is not fundamentally political, economic, or social – the challenge is fundamentally spiritual.

What we see as a power struggle – a struggle for political power, wealth, and money; control over the world out there – is actually a power struggle for personal power, control of the world in here, within each of us. We keep focusing on the wrong thing. Because we misplace our focus, we keep making the same mistakes. Conquering the world – the environment, circumstances, and people – is not the way to harmony and prosperity; making the most of ourselves is.

What we see as an attempt to conquer the world out there is the manifestation of our failure to subdue the world in here, within ourselves. This is ultimately and fundamentally where we always go wrong.

Political, economic, and social turmoil are what we experience when we fail to master ourselves. We lose our way. What we see in the system's failings are failings of our focus. We end up fighting over scraps out there when, in truth, we can have it all if we orient ourselves properly and get ourselves right – our attitude, understanding, and focus.

Reality would be profoundly different if we would focus on and accept the truth: **We are spiritual beings having a physical experience.** It is not "*us against the world.*" We have the opportunity to explore and experience, learn and grow, create and contribute together, to express more life.

Unfortunately, we often lose our way. Seemingly lost and alone in what we perceive as a dangerous world, we seek power. We strive to control the world out there. We mistakenly put power over principle – over truth – and the trouble begins.

Here in the United States, both political parties Republican and Democrat, are tools used by the few to take from the many. The political parties are instruments used to compete; power instruments used to dominate and control people. The game of politics is power: control over the world out there, control of other people. As a competitive game, there are few winners and many losers. Ultimately, played this way – for external power – politics is a losing game.

Power corrupts. And due to the corrosive nature of power, the powerful always succumb and abuse power.

ARE POLITICIANS INEPT?

The answer to my second deliberately provocative question: "***Are politicians really this inept?***" is also yes **and** no.

Politicians are human beings overcome by the weight and conditions of this physical reality. At some point, they embrace a mission to compete for power. What the people see as incompetence and corruption are politicians playing a game with few rules and one objective: to seize and secure power. How the politicians achieve that objective is of little consequence. The single-minded objective of the game is to win.

A few cunning competitors hire politicians for a very specific purpose: to consolidate power. American politicians have proven to be masters of the game. As most Americans are not benefitting from politicians' work, most Americans consider politicians inept. This is by design. Politicians take from the many to enrich the few – as they are hired to do. Determining whether politicians are inept depends on where you stand. If you are among the cunning few, politicians are extremely capable; some might say 'stable geniuses.' If you are among the many, politicians are corrupt and inept.

In a democratic republic where, in theory, the power rests with the people, my bias is toward the people. It is us, the people, who let this abuse happen.

Delusions, fear, and hate dominate American politics. Through ignorance and misguided self-indulgence, we have cast a once great nation, an aspirational nation founded on inspiring ideals, into a dismal state.

We Americans love to wrap ourselves in the flag and say how great we are. *'We are number one.'* It is time we recognize we are not number one in any category anyone should aspire to be number one in.

The coronavirus debacle and an attack on democracy perpetrated by a sitting president, a political party of enablers, and a hateful mob speak for themselves. Now, beyond the obvious...

We have accumulated more debt than any nation in human history. We are racing toward thirty trillion, with a "T," dollars of federal debt. Debt is a tax on the future; play now – pay later.

We Americans say, *'It is not a tax we will have to pay – it's on our kids and grandkids. Too bad for them.'*

To understand how fast we are accelerating to greatness, consider that the 2017-2021 Trump administration, in four years, accumulated more debt more quickly than any previous administration in U.S. history. You have to love those conservative, fiscally responsible Republicans. Democrats never claimed to be fiscally responsible, so the debt orgy continues as the Biden administration seeks to break Trump's record. Add state and local government debt and pile on an additional five-plus trillion dollars.

But wait, you say, that thirty-five-plus trillion and counting is government debt, "*That doesn't matter.*" Our personal debt – mortgages, credit cards, auto, and student loans - amounts to another sixteen trillion. And I have yet to mention corporate and financial debt and unfunded obligations. Debt is a ball and chain. Play now, pay later. 'America is number one.'

Finance: what once was a supporting component of the economy – enabling the real economy: infrastructure, transportation, communication, energy, manufacturing, and so on; finance now comprises one-fifth of the U.S. economy. And finance is a closed system. We print money as fast as possible to enrich the few further. Thousands of people dying every day from Covid-19, and the stock market surges higher. Insurrection, and the stock market surges higher. 'We are doing great.'

We are running a trade deficit of more than eight hundred billion dollars a year. Print more money, get more stuff.

While the government reports unemployment hovering near six percent, we now have more than one hundred million able-bodied American adults sitting on the sidelines outside the labor force.

The government tells us the inflation rate is experiencing a minor but temporary blip. The real inflation rate for things you actually need and buy exceeds ten percent.

We have forty-five million American families on food stamps.

Two out of three American adults are overweight or obese.

One in three American adults are addicted to poison: cigarettes, drugs, and alcohol.

We use more drugs in America for everything from recreation to weight loss to stress relief to actually treating disease than any other country by leaps and bounds.

Our health system represents close to twenty percent of GDP. Per capita, we spend more than every other developed nation in the world by a wide margin. And except in a few areas, we get terrible results. Our healthcare system itself, in a typical non-pandemic year, is the third leading cause of death in America.

Life expectancy is on a downward trajectory. Suicides and deaths of despair are growing at alarming rates. 'We're number one.'

Right now, the United States has more than two million three hundred thousand men, women, and children behind bars. The United States has assembled nearly one-quarter of all imprisoned human beings on the planet.

On a *Freedom Index* ranking all countries based on such factors as rule of law, security, rights, sound money, and so on, the United States does not even break the top fifteen. 'We are doing great.'

Transparency International, a global coalition against corruption, ranked the United States as twenty-third. In the neighborhood of Bhutan and Chile. More corrupt than the United Arab Emirates. And we are sinking in those rankings fast.

If that is not enough, now the big one:

Healthy, productive, prosperous relationships, communities and societies are built on a foundation of trust. With an assault on truth, the United States, at home and abroad, ranks among the least trusted and trustworthy of all major nations globally. Less trustworthy than China, India, and Saudi Arabia by wide margins and even Argentina. We are rolling in the muck with such stalwarts of trust and integrity as Russia.

Plato once observed, "Whatever deceives men seems to produce a magical enchantment." Americans are undoubtedly enchanted as they are greatly deceived.

Thirty years ago, I read a prediction that the United States would stand alone as a pariah nation on the world stage. I did not believe it, but now here we are. Welcome to America in 2021.

We, these United States, are in a mess, a mess. The state of our union is precarious at best.

Americans fundamentally misunderstand politics. Unless we carefully guard against human nature, politics always becomes a game of taking from the many to enrich the few.

Awash in lies, the many are easily deceived and pitted against one another. Divide and conquer is the political strategy. Fear and hate are the political weapons.

Knowing we love to play the victim, politicians, masters of misdirection, spin people up over hot-button social and economic issues: immigrants, guns, abortion, race, taxes, while the few consolidate wealth and power. It is working great. Every man for himself. People gladly jump on the fear and hate victim-bandwagon. It gives them someone to blame.

I will tell you who is to blame: us, we Americans. There it is. There is the unvarnished truth.

The decline of the United States is accelerating because of us – because we, the people, refuse to see what is happening right before our eyes. Instead of facing the fact that succeeding is up to us – all of us together – we play the victim and run from responsibility.

We forfeit our power. We give it away. Because the responsibility of power is too great for most of us to bear. We give power to the bold and the cunning so we do not have to be responsible – we can blame someone else.

We are not making America great again.

So, let us figure out first what is going on. And then let us get to the truth. If we cannot deal with the truth, we deserve whatever we get.

PART I

WHAT THE HECK IS GOING ON?

CHAPTER 1

SPINNING OUT OF CONTROL

*A*re you concerned about what is happening right now?

We have a worldwide pandemic, but even as the pandemic subsides as vaccines are produced and widely distributed, turmoil is evident practically everywhere. The virus added fuel to a burning fire. People are struggling financially as the American and world economies teeter on the edge of solvency. Social relations are adversarial and ugly as more and more people embrace fear and hate politics in an effort to get theirs.

Things are spinning out of control. What the heck is going on?

CONSENSUS?

I don't know what drew you to this manuscript. Sometimes, I feel like I am the only person who thinks like I do. Perhaps not.

I wrote a book a few years ago called ***Success 101: How Life Works – Know the Rules, Play to Win***. That book focuses on improving lives – yours, mine, everyone's. The premise of ***Success 101: How Life Works*** is that you ultimately hold the cards. You are in charge of your own life and how it plays out, for better or worse, for good or for ill; **mostly**, but not absolutely. Something greater than "self" is in play.

The emphasis and focus of ***Success 101: How Life Works*** is optimistic. You have power, and your choices matter. This book, ***Are Americans Really this Stupid?*** accepts that hopeful, personal-power truth. It is, however, an attempt to understand and frame in context why so many refuse to employ their power for good.

Are environmental, economic, political, and social forces so overwhelming? Or is it something else, something much more pervasive and fundamental?

You see, if we – you and I – are ultimately in charge of our own lives, for better or worse, then this time of turmoil is a call to action, a call to change. It is **not** time to relinquish responsibility as so many do. Now is precisely the time to lean in and take charge of your life.

I attempt to be objective in this book, but having read this far, you have likely recognized my biases. Think of my perspective this way: I say, "All of me is God, but I'm not all of God." Some will say heresy. Hear me out. Something greater is at work in our lives and in life.

Throughout this manuscript, I mention opposing forces and spectrums or continuums repeatedly.

Is it nature or nurture that guides us?

Or something in between?

Are you powerful or powerless?

Or something in between?

Do you chart your own course, or do others chart your course for you?

Or something in between?

We can observe the health of individuals and society on one spectrum or through one contrast: **an internal or an external focus**. The dichotomy driving the conflagration that is *our time* is a "***me***" or a "***we***" focus.

As social beings, strength comes from unity. United, we can accomplish much. Divided, we quarrel, fight, and ultimately fall. As we proceed through life, individuals and society constantly move between an ***I-me-my*** focus and a ***we-us-together*** focus. As we mature, we recognize and realize, "It's not all about me."

At its extreme, a "***me***" focus says only one thing matters: me. 'My sole concern is how the environment and other people impact or affect me. It is me against the world.'

A "***we***" focus, on the other hand, sees from a broader vantage point. 'I am not all that is or all that matters. I am part of a community, an environment, and a world. Everything I do affects others, and everything others do affects me. We are all in this together.' While ultimately, we control our focus and perspective, the crowd and other people influence us positively and negatively.

CHANGE & BALANCE

Through ***Are Americans Really this Stupid?*** we will not consider life from a physics, thermodynamics, chemical, or biological perspective. We will view life from a spiritual, psychological, and social perspective.

Let us establish some common ground by acknowledging two primary factors: change and balance.

Everything in our awareness, everything we taste, touch, see, smell, and hear, everything we sense and feel, is in constant motion. We are moving this very instant. What is still, calm, and steady is really moving. The one constant of experience is change.

Slowing ourselves down does not stop the motion; it does not stop change. Everything changes all the time. The best we can do is make sense of that motion and influence change. Everything is changing. Change is our one constant. How we deal with change matters.

Life is speeding up and becoming more chaotic. This chaos is why we ask, "What the heck is going on?"

Like fish have no concept of water, most people have no idea of life beyond the boundaries of their senses. Life just happens. We keep moving. Things keep changing, and we deal with it.

Sometimes, we feel good. Occasionally, we do not. We keep striving to feel better. Once we do feel better, we want things to stop changing and moving. Like Goldilocks, we do not want to be too hot or too cold, too big or too small, too fast or too slow – we want things just right. We want life to be in equilibrium – **in balance**. And once it is – in balance, comfortable – we want things to remain as they are.

But life does not work that way. Things change.

And we; think about it; most of us hate change. We resist change. And that – resisting change – is a good part of our problem.

Life moves in cycles. Like a pendulum, life swings toward balance, then beyond it until it reaches an extreme, then swings back. The chaos we are experiencing now is life at an extreme: the chaos and crisis phase of the social cycle.

An extreme is a transition period. We have gone too far embracing *every-man-for-himself, it's-all-about-me.* Now, we must change direction and come together. We must swing away from "***me***" back toward "***we***" again.

Are Americans Really this Stupid? is an attempt to help you take **control** of your own life and in so doing, help **us all** move in a more productive direction.

I use "**control**" very deliberately: take **control** of **your life**. Taking control of **your** life is essential to **our** changing direction.

TWO PARTS

Are Americans Really this Stupid? is presented in two parts. Through this part, ***Part I***, we focus on what motivates individuals and what moves the collective. We explore how "***me***" impacts "***we***."

In ***Part 2***, we focus on the truth about American politics – the practical motivations that manifest in our economics, social lives, and our power dynamics.

First, we head back to nature.

CHAPTER 2

BACK TO NATURE

God created the world in six days. On the seventh day, God rested.

We must begin at the source to understand what is going on by exploring what makes us us. Getting our minds around what is going on requires understanding why we do what we do.

This universe, galaxy, solar system, and world all operate within certain parameters, which scientists call laws. We have energy. Energy collects to form mass – matter. We have gravity, thermodynamics, and so on – forces acting in dynamic opposition. The opposition, the ebb and flow, generates synergy and cycles. Life operates in cycles.

A fundamental feature of life is that it intends to grow. An organizing force draws energy together. That energy combines and arranges into what we call organisms. Organisms draw on and collect more energy, multiply and develop. Life intends to grow.

We will explore more about the cooperative nature of nature, but for now, let us peel back the onion on human nature.

THREE BRAINS

In his 1859 book *On the Origin of Species*, Charles Darwin theorized that life evolves. Darwin stated that all species of organisms arise and develop through the natural selection of minor, inherited variations that increase the individual's ability to compete, survive, and reproduce.

Guiding behaviors or instincts are encoded within animals and augmented by parental modeling. Humans, like all creatures, have instincts. Instincts are those behaviors encoded into our DNA to compete, survive, and reproduce.

Two pervasive and powerful instincts help us survive. The first of these is fear. A threat, an environmental threat, say, being near the edge of a cliff or a threat from an animal or another person, generates fear. Fear excites energy within, ultimately guiding us to respond in one of three ways: freeze, flee, or fight. Fear is our primary survival instinct. In a dangerous environment, those who do not fear do not survive.

That second pervasive and powerful guiding instinct is the need to conserve energy.

Living is an exercise in energy management. We need energy to survive and thrive. But usable energy is not always and everywhere readily accessible, so we must conserve energy. Conserving energy is a primary survival strategy, a survival instinct.

Our typical means to conserve energy is our habits process; more on that in a minute. But first, something besides instinct drives and guides us.

We can divide human beings' control centers, our brains, into three parts. The first is known as the reptilian aspect of the brain. The reptilian portion of our brain – the brain stem or hindbrain – regulates bodily functions, from respiration to circulation and digestion to our immune system. The brain stem operates mainly in the background without conscious intervention. The reptilian brain is where survival instincts reside.

The second of our three parts of the brain is our mammalian brain. The limbic system, found between the brain stem and the cerebral hemispheres, governs emotion and manages memory. This is also the part of the brain that drives most of our decision-making.

"Not so fast." You say, "Emotions don't drive our decision-making."

Don't they?

EMOTION DRIVES US

We human beings like to believe we are conscious, deliberate decision-makers and use our brains' highest functions to make decisions. But that is rarely the case. We kid ourselves.

We delude ourselves into believing when we confront a situation, before we choose a course of action, before we act, we go through a deliberate decision-making process. The delusion says we consider options thoughtfully, weigh pros and cons, and evaluate potential outcomes. Then, we choose the best course of action for that circumstance.

Circumstance to thought to action. Or so we say. This is **not**, **not** how we make decisions and act.

What typically, usually, mostly happens is we find ourselves in a situation. That situation causes energy to flow, what we feel as emotion. In response to emotion, we act. ***Circumstance to feeling to action.***

We do not thoughtfully consider options. If we do think at all, our thinking is usually to justify our emotional response.

We human beings do not like to think. Thinking takes too much energy and effort. Remember that instinct to conserve energy?

To minimize thinking, we rely on habit. Habits are automatic action sequences we adopt in response to familiar cues to get specific rewards. Sixty percent of everything we do daily, we do habitually, automatically, to conserve energy.

Whereas most creatures operate by instinct alone, we make most of our choices – we decide what we will do by way of emotions. Most of which we have committed to habit. Emotions rule our decision-making.

I have presented two component aspects of our brains: the reptilian and the mammalian parts. The brain's third or higher functioning capacity – what happens in our cerebral hemispheres, the neocortex – is what we refer to as intellect or reason or, more appropriately, thought. Conscious thought is our ability to project ourselves through time and space and examine circumstances and ideas from different and diverse perspectives.

Thought, conscious or unconscious, is the bridge between the physical reality of automatic biological functioning, instinct and emotion, and mind. Mind is an undefined and undefinable dimension, commonly referred to as spirit. The highest function of our brains is communicating with mind – the dimension of spirit.

We will dive further into that dimension of spirit, but we have more foundation to pour.

MIGHT MAKES RIGHT

Herbert Spencer, a contemporary of Charles Darwin, coined the phrase "survival of the fittest" and went on to frame what became "Social Darwinism." The theory of survival of the fittest adhered to the golden rule: not the "*Do unto others as you would have them do unto you*" version of the golden rule, but rather the "*He who has the gold makes the rules*." He who has the power, the power to rule, rules.

Social Darwinism – survival of the fittest – is a philosophy of ***might makes right***. Power prevails. Those who dominate, by design, should dominate, and are right in doing so. Nature establishes that those who survive should survive – and that might is the only legitimate moral authority. ***Might makes right* – which always results in the many serving the few – has been and is the dominant operating principle of humankind.** It is the reality of competing in nature.

Only the winners write history books.

We will examine this idea of survival of the fittest further, however, now, we seek truth.

CHAPTER 3

KNOW THE TRUTH

In the last chapter, we discussed the Darwinian notion of "*survival of the fittest.*" While this idea has immense implications for getting a handle on what is happening, let us see if we can illuminate a truth.

I have a question for you:

What motivates you? What moves you? What causes you to act?

You have likely heard of Abraham Maslow, the 20th Century American psychologist best known for devising a human hierarchy of needs.

Base-level needs in Maslow's hierarchy are physiological or survival essentials like food, water, shelter, and clothing. The next level of needs are safety and security. We need food and water immediately; then, we want to make it to our next meal.

After safety and security are social needs: belongingness and love. We are social beings. Youngsters can only survive with older, more experienced, capable people looking out for them. As humans mature, we seek to fit in and ultimately secure a place for ourselves amongst a group. The fourth level in Maslow's hierarchy of needs is esteem or status. Once we feel we belong, we ascend the pecking order, gaining power.

The culminating level in Maslow's hierarchy, the level above esteem and status, is what he termed self-actualization: realizing and achieving an individual's purpose.

Needs are critical to survival, as Maslow determined. But we also have other motivators, what we label *wants*. Wants stem from the environment, opportunities, and personal and social tendencies and preferences.

LET'S SIMPLIFY

Life, as is its nature, presents us with circumstances, obstacles, hurdles, or challenges. Some people, most people, well all people at times, interpret circumstances as difficulties that cause discomfort and pain.

We prefer pleasure to pain, so we often avoid or move away from life's challenges rather than deal with them. We tend to move toward what feels good – what we find pleasurable – and move away from what we find displeasing, uncomfortable, or painful.

When we are hungry and thirsty, we feel discomfort. The solution to our discomfort is to eat and drink. Ridding ourselves of hunger is pleasing. We seek pleasure and avoid pain. But life is more complicated than just feeding ourselves. Life holds much more potential.

LIVING IS FEELING

We can reduce living to one thing, one word. We live to **feel.**

Everything we do, we do to feel. No exceptions. Life, this experience of life is a feeling adventure. We explore and experience, learn and grow, create and contribute, and we feel through all of it. As we express life, we feel.

And we constantly strive to feel better. We want to feel good.

The highest good is what Aristotle determined to be the purpose of life: to be happy. Happiness, akin to flourishing, is the ultimate pleasure – the feeling we ultimately desire.

The feelings we feel come from one source: our minds. Our minds manage energy. The energy we feel in our bodies is emotion. Interpreting external stimuli and thoughts, our minds spark emotions – feelings.

Most of us assume the thoughts we think and the emotions we feel are products of our physical environment and circumstances. We tend to believe what we feel, and how we feel results from what the world and others around us present. Whatever emotion we feel, whatever level of energy we sense in our bodies, good, bad, or indifferent, is the result of something out there; is caused by something out there. In reality, what we feel is always and only the result of our interpretation of what we perceive out there.

The need, want, or desire to feel motivates and moves us to act.

Most of us refuse to believe we can manage what we feel through our thoughts. Most people believe feelings are a product of external circumstances or the environment. Whatever is out there – obstacles, hurdles, challenges – causes us to feel whatever we feel in here. That just is **not** so.

Managing our feelings through thought is the only real power we have. And our power of thought is the only power we need.

Ninety-eight or ninety-nine percent of people deny responsibility for how they feel. Most people believe external conditions determine, cause, or generate feelings. And since external conditions – obstacles, hurdles, challenges, difficulties – cause discomfort, the way to gain control over feelings is to gain control over external circumstances. Competing is the solution we embrace.

This is a critical factor in determining what the heck is going on.

THE PLEASURE / PAIN CONTINUUM

Consider pleasure and pain as a continuum. On one end of the spectrum is pleasure; on the other is pain.

Life presents circumstances. We tend to move toward pleasure and away from pain. But, as we know, life is not as simple as that.

Most people do not believe they control their feelings when dealing with difficulties. They believe external circumstances – those difficulties – cause them to feel good, bad, or indifferent. This belief causes more problems. It is a distorted view of reality, a mistaken belief about how life works.

"Since external stuff makes me feel – getting more control over external stuff will give me control over how I feel."

Again, this is **not** how things work.

It is not that the energy of circumstances does not affect us – it does. It is that we get ourselves into circumstances. And we choose what we focus on and how we interpret those circumstances. We have more power and control than most people ever realize. Our choices lead to our feelings.

We have control over our own minds to the degree that we can overcome those negative impulses of instinct and emotion. While some believe the power of instinct and emotion is absolute, the reality is that we determine what we think and how we feel. Instinct and emotion have their place – to guide and assist – but allowing negative instinct and emotion to dominate undermines our ability to choose, keeping us from living full lives.

Most people, really the vast majority, refuse to believe the truth. **Your ability to think is your power**, your means to affect how you feel. Instead of accepting the truth, most people contend, to the bitter end, that it is external forces and the instincts and emotions those external forces illicit that determine how they feel.

KNOW THE TRUTH

You are familiar with the adage: **Know the truth, and the truth will set you free.**

The most powerful of human truths is ***you control how you feel***. Only once you accept – **know** and **believe** this truth will you be free.

You control how you feel.

In our first few chapters, we determined:

- Life is in motion. Change is the one constant.
- Life moves in cycles.
- We are on a **feeling** adventure. We live to feel.
- Our interpretation of circumstances determines how we feel.
- Instinct, emotion, and thought all motivate people. However, while **our ability to think is our most incredible power**, instinct and emotion prevail for most people.
- Most of us refuse to believe we are in control of our lives, and therefore, most of us refuse to **think**. Most tend to believe whatever is out there determines how they feel. So, to gain control of how they feel, people seek to gain control of external circumstances.
- Refusing to accept the truth that we determine how we feel, people bind themselves. They imprison themselves and yet still yearn to be free.

Next, we delve deeper into personal power.

CHAPTER 4

YOU'VE GOT THE POWER

I hope we are not getting too intense, and you are enjoying our exploration of truth. I suspect you are. Otherwise, you would not still be reading. We are going to arrive, I assure you, at a simple and understandable conclusion.

KNOW THE TRUTH AND THE TRUTH WILL SET YOU FREE

The United States of America was established and built on the ideal of liberty. Everyone yearns to be free. But what exactly does freedom mean?

Many people will tell you, "Freedom means being able to do what I want to do when I want." For most, the personal definition of freedom is a "***me***" definition. "I want absolute freedom; the ability to do what I want, when I want, where I want, with whatever I want, despite consequences." Freedom is all about "***me***."

Every force has an opposing force, a contrasting side. Everything has a cost. On the flip side of the *coin of freedom* is **responsibility**.

Freedom always comes with responsibility. It is impossible to divorce freedom from responsibility. Yet we human beings try and try and try. We want freedom – the ability to do what we want, when we want – without regard to consequences. Consequences are what we are responsible for.

Just like realizing we determine how we feel, we must realize **freedom is not free**. Freedom has consequences. And unless and until we accept the burden of those consequences – bear the responsibility that comes with freedom – we will never be free.

Freedom without responsibility is an adolescent pipedream, a fallacy, an illusion; it is getting something for nothing. That is **not** the way life works.

You might think: 'The burdens are starting to add up.'

Life is a dynamic place, a dynamic adventure. As we move through life, we feel. What we feel, ultimately, is determined by our most extraordinary power, our greatest strength – our **ability to think**. Yet most people find this idea, this truth – that they control their own feelings – repulsive. We refuse to know the truth. Instead, we long for freedom without consequence, freedom without responsibility.

We dig ourselves quite a hole.

Are you getting a sense of what the heck is going on? And it is not about **them** and what is **out there**. It is about **us** and what is **in here – inside us**.

PAINTING A PICTURE

We will keep moving forward, but we have yet to paint the whole picture.

Remember our pleasure–pain continuum?

Opposing forces are always active. We want to feel good and not feel bad, so we move toward pleasure and away from pain. Even when we feel good, however, the discomfort of fear often arises, giving us the insecure feeling that we could lose what we have.

Since most people believe external circumstances determine how they feel, then by controlling external circumstances, they can control how they feel. If only they were free to do what they want when they want, "When **I** am free to do what **I** want when **I** want; then **I** will be happy."

Our solution to the mistake of believing we do not control how we feel; we do not have personal power; is to attempt to control what is out there. "If I gain control of external circumstances: stuff, people, the environment – everything out there; I can control how I feel, and I can be happy."

"Control – power – will get me out of the hole I've dug." That is what we believe. Getting control over others is the answer.

A POWER TRIANGLE

Create an image in your mind's eye. Envision that pleasure–pain continuum as a line. On the right is pleasure; on the left, pain. Now, add another dimension to your image. Create an equilateral triangle. On the base is the pleasure–pain continuum, and on the peak of your triangle is power.

"To break the tension between pleasure and pain, all I need is power; then I can control how I feel." Seeking power becomes our paramount concern.

Most people believe gaining the power they lack will solve their problems.

They forget or deny they already possess personal power – all the power they need. And that they are free to do what they want if they are willing to bear the burden of responsibility.

This denial – denying their power – is unfortunate for us all.

The truth is **you control how you feel**. You already possess personal power – your ability to think. Most people are not willing to accept this reality.

"If I have power, then I am responsible." This is too great a burden to bear. Most people want to control circumstances, people, and things. Most want something for nothing: freedom without responsibility. We forfeit personal power to pursue, as if our lives depend on it, control over others.

Go back to the image you created in your mind. That image of a triangle represents the pleasure–pain continuum on the base and power at the peak.

We want to feel pleasure, feel good, and we want to avoid pain. Through all our struggles, we believe the way to get control of this entire process – to once and for all control how we feel – is by controlling everything out there. We seek power, the ability to control others and circumstances as the solution to our problems. The challenge is, however, there is no such thing as something for nothing. Everything has a cost.

Think of your image. If you abandon the pleasure–pain continuum, leave the base, and move toward power; you give up something. A tradeoff is the cost of choosing. We rationalize that by seeking power, we are forfeiting some pleasure and enduring some pain temporarily. This is an essential, temporary, acceptable tradeoff, a necessary evil. We rationalize that once we have power, we will have absolute control over whether we feel pleasure or pain. But the truth is we put ourselves on a treadmill. We constantly struggle through an endless cycle, moving from power to pleasure to pain over and over again.

YOU ALREADY ARE POWERFUL

Remember, before you got sidetracked in your quest for control, you already had personal power. You have personal power now – all the power you need.

We are here, living, experiencing this adventure, to express life. We are here not for "**me**" – not me alone. We are here for "**we**" – us together, all of us, and all that is. We are here to express more life together.

We get caught. We fall into the trap of "self." We make being happy our primary concern. And we believe that to be happy, we need more control over what is out there.

We focus on the wrong thing. Happiness is not the ultimate objective: a prize to seize, an endpoint or objective. Happiness is a by-product of something else. You have the power. We all possess power. We need to use our power appropriately. Instead, however, we start to make progress, then, too often, forfeit our power.

CHAPTER 5

FORFEITING OUR POWER

Do you want to know what the heck is going on?

The truth is you have power, I have power, we all have power. The chaos and the turmoil rampant in society today is the result of our refusal to accept and employ **our** personal power for the collective good.

We refuse to believe that we control our own lives and how we feel. If we accept that we are in charge, we must accept the burden of responsibility that comes along with being in charge. Rather than accept personal power and responsibility, we compete for control over others. We seek freedom without responsibility, something for nothing.

Accepting responsibility also illuminates that ***I am responsible for more than just me***. I am accountable to others, us collectively, the environment, and the world. A prospect most of us fear or find burdensome.

AN EXERCISE TO COMPLETE

Get together with a friend. Do not do this on a whim. You must frame this properly; otherwise, you will annoy your friend.

The task is to uncover what your friend really wants.

Ask your friend, "What do you want?"

The first, immediate answer is usually something flip or simple or transparent. But you are going to go deep – seven layers deep. If this person is willing to deep-dive with you, ask them why they want what they want. Then, keep going.

"Why do you want that?" and keep going.

The deeper you go, the more revealing the inquiry becomes. By the seventh level of asking why, you are usually down to what that person really wants.

Some people, rather than stepping down level by level, will conclude they want to be happy. Getting to happy, though, usually takes you through stuff, people, events, and accomplishments – external things that people believe ultimately provide happiness.

This can be a compelling exercise.

People will say they want stuff – houses, cars, and toys of all kinds. They will say they want relationships – connection with others. And they will say they want experiences – achievements, the ability to travel, and so on. They have different reasons and motivations for what they want, but it all leads back to feeling good and being happy.

REJECTING OUR POWER

In simple terms, we all say we want more stuff, more relationships, more experiences – more life. That is precisely what life is for: to explore and experience, learn and grow, create and contribute, all to express more life. Why, then, can't we get along and cooperatively and collaboratively express more life?

The answer rests in our fundamental mistake of not accepting and embracing our personal power.

Every force has an opposing force. Every asset represents a liability. Every acquisition has a cost. Every gift comes with a burden.

We, you and I, possess personal power. We can direct our lives and determine, for the most part, where we go, what we do, and how we feel. Accepting personal power is knowing the truth and setting ourselves free. However, that freedom personal power allows comes with a cost, a burden. That burden, that cost, is responsibility.

If we ultimately control our own lives, we must accept responsibility for what is, for what we do and do not do, for what we accomplish and where we fall short. Responsibility is uncomfortable. It can be painful. It demands effort.

Responsibility is the cost accompanying power, the pain that comes with the pleasure of freedom. We would rather avoid pain. So we reject responsibility.

In the *Book of Genesis*, Chapter 3, God asks the man if he ate from the forbidden tree. The man blames the woman. And the woman blames the serpent. From the beginning, we have denied responsibility. Instead of assuming our power, we forfeit that personal power. We give it away. We stake our futures on external circumstances and controlling others.

THE 80-20 RULE

Are you familiar with the Pareto Principle?

It is commonly known as the Eighty-Twenty Rule.

The Eighty-Twenty Rule recognizes that some things matter more than others and that some causes generate outsized results. Not that 80-20 is an absolute ratio, but typically, twenty percent of things matter, and eighty percent do not.

Have you ever noticed that you wear twenty percent of your clothing about eighty percent of the time? That twenty percent of roadways carry eighty percent of traffic? That twenty percent of the population controls eighty percent of the world's wealth?

A vital few things matter. The trivial many do not.

I bring up wealth and the concentration of wealth because most people want more, more stuff, more things, and more experiences. And to get those, they seek more money.

Why do relatively few have so much while so many have so little in a world of such opulence?

Even if you eliminate the COVID-19 pandemic from consideration, you have probably noticed growing discontent around America and the world. When we experience economic turmoil, political and social turmoil follow. Why is that?

In a world of more than enough for everyone, why are so many Americans and people all around the globe embracing the politics of fear and hate?

LIFE CYCLES

We know life moves through cycles and have seen this cycle before. The pendulum has swung away from "***we***" toward "***me***"; from accepting personal power and responsibility toward rejecting personal power and responsibility.

We have reached the every-man-for-himself extreme again, where "me – me – me; me first" is the order of the day. We are fighting for control. It is survival of the fittest in the jungles of time and space. At this extreme, we must decide either to commit suicide, destroying what we have built and ending the cycle, or to claim our power and bear the burden of responsibility turning ourselves in a new direction, a better direction – together.

How did we get from individuals forfeiting their power to a worldwide mess?

Through that combination of human nature and the nature of power.

We humans have uniquely powerful gifts but also glaring vulnerabilities. On the one hand, we possess the ***ability to think***, allowing us to change perspectives, travel through time, and bridge to the realm of mind and spirit. On the other hand, we must deal with instincts of ***fear*** and the ***need to conserve***

energy. And being social by nature, we are susceptible to the influence of others – for better or for worse.

It only takes twenty percent of people getting on board to swing the pendulum one way or the other. As life changes and the pendulum swings, social influence accelerates our advance or decline.

Is it the nature of power that is the corroding influence or something else?

CHAPTER 6

POWER CORRUPTS

Physical reality conforms to the "*law of the jungle*," "*survival of the fittest*," "*might makes right*."

Though grounded in physical reality, we human beings originate from another dimension. **We are spiritual beings having a physical experience.** We possess boundless potential, an endless capacity to explore and experience, learn and grow, create and contribute – all to fulfill the intent of living: **To express more life.**

The power we possess has a purpose. Personal power allows us to fulfill our highest and truest potential.

Facing the power-driven jungle's challenges, we struggle to find our way. We individually and collectively grapple with power. The greater the struggle, the more chaos we experience.

What is it about power? What makes this power struggle so wrenching?

WHO ACCEPTS THE POWER

Human beings have unique and incredible abilities. The power those abilities imply is best used collectively – in unity – cooperatively and collaboratively with others. We can, however, direct that awe-inspiring power toward divisive, destructive ends. The "*law of the jungle*" reduces survival to power. Survival, progress, and prosperity come down to how we manage power.

The ancient Chinese concept of Ying and Yang advises a cosmic duality governs the universe. Two sets of opposing and complementing forces or cosmic energies comprise our reality. Dealing with these opposing forces, we attempt to achieve a delicate balance. The pendulum constantly swings between "***we***" and "***me***" extremes.

We are experiencing life, having been bestowed gifts, capacities, and talents. These privileges, however, come at a cost. With personal power comes the burden of personal responsibility.

As we have discussed, when the pendulum swings toward "***me***" and away from "***we***," more and more people push back against the burden of responsibility. More and more of us abandon or forfeit our power. But what happens to that power?

That potential power is up for grabs by anyone willing to seize it. This is where the trouble begins.

Forgoing the burden of responsibility, we rely on external circumstances to determine our feelings instead of embracing power. Abandoning our power, we turn control over to others who tell us where to go, what to do, and how to feel.

But all power comes with responsibility. We cannot separate power from responsibility as hard as we try. Individuals who do not want to be responsible let someone else – someone willing to take on responsibility – control them. The security of confinement is more comforting than the unnerving prospect of freedom. This relinquishing of responsibility sets in motion a self-reinforcing cycle of assuming external circumstances and other people control our lives.

Ultimately, we can manage power in one of two ways. We can embrace our power and the responsibility that accompanies that power and, by accepting responsibility, set ourselves free. Or we can give our power away.

Coming to terms with power is a maturing process. While I am characterizing managing someone else's power as troubling, there are circumstances requiring that we manage other's power. Children must mature into their power. Power management within families falls to parents. Parents maintain power over and responsibility for their children. Children will not survive without a parent's care.

As children grow, good parents teach their children the extent and limits of their power and the responsibility that comes with it. Appropriately nurtured, upon reaching adulthood, an individual will fully embrace their power, with its attendant responsibility, to become a mature, fully empowered member of society.

Since personal power is the means for individuals to fulfill their potential and power comes with responsibility, only selfless people take on additional power willingly without malicious intent. Genuine leadership is assuming power freely given and bearing the weight of that additional responsibility for the sole purpose of helping individuals grow and become. **Authentic leadership is assisting others to achieve their true potential.** Good parents are genuine leaders.

Rather than embrace power, however, many pursue a different power management strategy. Wary of the responsibility power demands, many people attempt what they consider an easy, no responsibility, something for nothing, "***me first***," self-centered approach.

This no responsibility cycle can initiate within families. Parents denying they possess personal power teach their children that outside forces govern life and ultimately determine how they feel. Parents with this "I'm not responsible" worldview distort reality for their children. Children of parents who deny personal responsibility grow up learning to blame everyone and everything out there for their circumstances and how they feel. Never shouldering personal responsibility, children in these circumstances are taught that what matters is control over external circumstances and others. Survival demands putting "***me***" above everyone else.

People who do not accept personal power and responsibility – control over their feelings – focus on controlling others. Life is a *jungle*, and everything is a competition. These people compete with everyone, everywhere, all the time. In the *jungle*, people seek freedom without responsibility. They want something for nothing. And based on the economic, political, and social tactics routinely employed today, these people will do anything to get what they want. This is bad for us all.

We manage power by accepting responsibility for the consequences of our actions. Unfortunately, most people do not and will not admit they have power over their lives. It is not that everyone denies responsibility all the time. But it only takes twenty percent of the population to move an entire society positively or negatively. A few change the course of many.

When people forfeit their power and abandon personal responsibility, that power is up for grabs. We desperately struggle with power. We either accept personal power and the responsibility it demands or compete to gain control over circumstances and others. The struggle is very intimate and, right now, highly charged.

Personal power is a gift for an individual to achieve their true potential. Taking on another's power to advance one's self-interest is a misuse of power. The age-old adage is true: **Power corrupts, and absolute power corrupts absolutely.**

Personal power comes with a burden – responsibility – and that burden both exacts a price and offers a reward. The price is the consequences of choices we make. The reward is the freedom to choose.

Power people abandon is inherently corrosive. Personal power is meant for individuals to use to grow and mature and become. Over time, assuming additional responsibility, even a selfless person is tempted to turn from "***we***" to "***me***." Power corrupts, and absolute power corrupts absolutely.

The burden and grace of being human is embracing our power and accepting our responsibility to make the most of ourselves. Accepting your power makes all the difference.

CHAPTER 7

PEOPLE, POWER AND POLITICS

Shall we review?

A vital few things matter while the trivial many do not.

Personal power is just that, personal. And it is meant to help people realize their full potential.

We can exercise personal power, think, connect, collaborate, and create together, or we can compete against everyone, everywhere, all the time.

Personal power demands responsibility, a burden people often reject.

When a "***me***," "***me first***," or ***every-man-for-himself*** sentiment prevails, people seek to dominate and control others.

A "*me, me first*" world is a "*survival of the fittest*" world. Survival of the fittest means "*might makes right*," and *might makes right* always results in the many serving the few.

The nature of power is corrosive. Seizing others' power is destructive.

EXPAND TO "WE," TO FIGURE OUT WHAT THE HECK IS GOING ON

Through painful experiences, humans have learned and learned again, over millennia, that progress only comes when we work together for mutual benefit. When we connect, collaborate, and create society advances.

In our fast-paced, material-oriented society, however, losing that sense of our personal power is particularly easy. Bombarded by media messages and social influence, we believe success and happiness depend on controlling what is out there. We believe having more – of everything – is how we achieve happiness. And since money buys stuff, we want more money.

Money has become the ultimate proxy for power. And power is control over things, circumstances, and people. The more money someone has, the more people that person controls. Money represents power. The quest for power is on in a *me first* world.

Money facilitates trade: commerce and the functioning of markets.

The fundamental purpose of commerce or business is to create and exchange value – helping people get what they want. The exchange adds value for all parties engaging in a transaction. Everyone gets something of value, something they want. Commerce is a magical thing. We build economies through commerce. Helping others get what they want by adding value through business is life-affirming.

But as the sentiment shifts from "***we***" win-win exchanges to "***me first***" win-lose exchanges, getting more for myself, more money, more wealth, and therefore more power becomes the paramount concern.

Increasingly, we see business and market competition as war. And in war, there are casualties. Instead of being life-affirming, business becomes a means of acquiring power, dominating, and subjugating. Accumulating money becomes **me** competing for **my** piece of the pie. In a *survival of the fittest* world, gathering money becomes the path to getting what I want. External power is the goal. Money is the means. More money means more control over what I have, do, experience, and ultimately feel.

WE'VE BEEN HERE BEFORE

Thomas Hobbes, an English philosopher, in his 1651 book *Leviathan*, asserted that without a moral governing standard, only *the law of the jungle* applies. Without the courage to accept and use our power to connect with the universal mind, no moral governing standard applies.

Hobbes explains that the law of the jungle is "*survival of the fittest*," a "*war of all against all*" with no rules and no moderating principles. Hobbes characterized that ultra-competitive struggle as resulting in life being solitary, poor, nasty, brutish, and short.

In a material-oriented, *me first* society, the crumbling of personal finances is the rumblings of war.

The *Eighty-Twenty Rule* applies to competing. Select individuals have the assets, attributes, and motivation to compete – manipulate, coerce, intimidate, or dominate most effectively—the big, the strong, the fast, and the cunning rule the jungle. The best the masses, the eighty percent, can hope for is to align with winners. Competing alone is a losing proposition. To avoid losing, people band together and take sides.

As the stakes increase and more money comes into play, the competition evolves from adding value to gaining control. The war is on. Competitors learn as money accumulates, power concentrates. By manipulating economic and mass media social levers, competitors control the game of power politics. Politics, too, becomes war by another means.

The sixteenth-century Italian philosopher Niccolo Machiavelli determined that in politics, only power matters. This sounds increasingly like the jungle. Machiavelli advocated that the ends justify the means. In the jungle, only power matters. We see Machiavelli's sentiment playing out in our contemporary politics.

Right now, money and power are more concentrated than ever in history. The more power concentrates, the more personal finances become unhinged, and the more anxious people become. The influence of the power-hungry permeates and unsettles the masses. Here in the United States, that anxiety resulted in electing a president who unabashedly promotes a "*me first*" agenda. Millions upon millions enthusiastically jumped on board precisely the wrong train.

COMPETE TO SUBJUGATE

The men and women who compete well build armies and skillfully deploy their forces to overwhelm and subdue their foes. The masses, people lacking the skills, talents, and energy to compete for power, or those who are outmaneuvered and overwhelmed, succumb to the authority of men and women seizing power. Power concentrates, and the many come to serve the few. The corrosive nature of power manifests.

Looked at from one perspective, the entire process of people forfeiting their power and others seizing and concentrating that power is an abomination: an aberration, an abuse of power. However, it is a component of an ongoing life cycle. It is natural. Something more significant than you and me is in charge. The corrosive nature of concentrated power ushers in the decline and death of society – the end of a cycle. Death is a necessary step leading to rebirth.

Each phase of a life cycle has within it elements to advance. Growth follows birth. Maturity follows growth. Decline follows maturity. Death follows decline. And decay follows death. Then birth begins the cycle anew. The cycle continues from birth, growth, maturity, decline, death, and decay to rebirth, all for a purpose: to express more life.

Life presents situations: environmental difficulties and social challenges. When we cooperate and collaborate, we overcome problems and challenges and advance. If we continue to connect and collaborate, we grow and prosper. Prosperity, however, has within it the seeds for undoing progress. Prosperity allows a "***me***" sentiment to take root.

The "***me***" sentiment causes us to abandon our power. Relinquishing personal power, we compete for control: external power. We seek to control what is out there: things, circumstances, and people.

Our failure to embrace our power destroys us and ultimately sets the lesson up again. Difficulties and challenges have a purpose; they are the means to growth, fulfillment, and happiness.

Our challenge, your and my challenge, the challenge each of us must face, revolves around personal power and responsibility.

Do we accept personal power and responsibility to empower ourselves and society? Or do we reject personal power and responsibility and doom ourselves to perpetual struggle?

CHAPTER 8

ON PURPOSE

Here we are.

We set out to determine what the heck is going on. We worked from the micro to the macro through the seven previous chapters. We began with nature and instinct; in this last chapter, we bridged to the social: business and politics.

We may be cursed: we live in interesting times. We are experiencing economic, political, and social upheaval simultaneously.

We have reached the transition point of a cycle. The pendulum has swung to an extreme. Either the "*me culture*" will initiate a self-destruct sequence, and our current system will die, or we will embrace our power, overcome the "*me culture*" and advance.

SO EASILY MISLED

Rejecting personal power, Americans are overwhelmingly consumed by dollar-and-cent considerations.

In our material-oriented society, the more unstable our personal finances become, the more agitated and anxious we become, and the more likely we are to blame scapegoats and initiate counterproductive action.

In 2016, Americans elected a president who blamed immigrants, minorities, Muslims, women, foreigners, Chinese, Europeans, political opponents, and even people from his own party and administration who disagreed with his "*me first*" agenda. Given the right conditions, Americans are pretty easily manipulated and misled.

Why?

Are we genuinely powerless?

Is society a "*survival of the fittest*" and "*might makes right*" jungle?

Is life really all about power?

Life is all about power. But not in the way most people think.

What we see as corporate greed, graft, political corruption, and moral decay are all caused by the same thing. Our success in life, personally, individually, and collectively as a community and a society, comes down to how we manage power, our power, and the responsibility that attends to that power.

My and your success as individuals, and our success as a society depend on each of us accepting and applying our power and responsibility. We must use our power for our growth and development. When we use power productively – when we apply and cultivate our power – we take responsibility for and serve the greater good. This expansive use of power benefits everyone.

OUR PURPOSE

Our task in living is to express more life, express the fullness of life. We are meant to realize the promise and fulfill our potential. That is why we are here. "All of you is God, but you are not all of God." Something greater than us is in charge.

So, how do we find our way amid all the chaos and struggle, the greed and the graft, the angst and turmoil?

We find our way **by living on purpose with faith.**

If you believed that physical reality is all there is – and that we are in the jungles of time and space to compete, survive, and reproduce – I do not think you would be reading this now. The challenges are trying, and the difficulties are real. But those challenges and difficulties have a purpose. You, I, and everyone else are meant to be happy.

You know and believe that. It is a matter of faith.

You are powerful. You get to decide what you think, what you say, where you go, what you do, and how you feel. You have the power.

Our challenge – the challenge every human being must confront – is to take up our cross, bear the burden of personal responsibility, and exercise our power.

Think. Connect with the infinite mind. Connect with God. The yoke is not heavy; the burden is light.

Happiness is not something to pursue. Happiness is not something we catch. Happiness is the by-product of living purposefully and giving our gifts away.

Our purpose is not to compete and survive. **Our purpose is to express more life.**

You express more life by employing that unique set of gifts you possess. By owning and employing your power, you are not a victim of circumstance. Using your power, you do not succumb to the struggle of the jungle. You have a more significant reason for being. You are meant to live on purpose. You are meant to fulfill your true potential and, in so doing, **be happy.**

Share what you have been given: your gifts, talents, skills, and abilities. Living on purpose is making the most of yourself. Use your strengths, talents, skills, and abilities to their most extraordinary ends. This is your purpose.

LIVE ON PURPOSE

Remember that equilateral triangle I had you imagine, with pain and pleasure on the base and power at the peak? Most people lose themselves in the endless struggle of moving from power to pleasure to pain again and again.

In your mind's eye lay that image flat. Add another dimension. Imagine a pyramid with purpose at the peak. The equilateral triangle, the struggle, is the base. Remove yourself from the struggle by **focusing on the peak – your purpose.**

Life is in motion. Life is change. You face challenges and encounter difficulties. This adventure features challenges and problems, pleasure and pain. Yet, you have the power. Use it. Feel the fullness of life.

Use your most incredible ability – your power to think, pray, meditate, and contemplate. **Listen to the still, small voice within.** Connect with your true source. Explore and experience, learn and grow, create and contribute to express more life.

By living on purpose you feel truly alive.

SO, WHAT THE HECK IS GOING ON?

Aristotle said happiness is the aim of life. Socrates said, "An unexamined life is not worth living." Socrates' notion is that most people never find their purpose. They waste their lives struggling with pleasure, power, and pain.

That is what's going on.

What the heck is going on is that **we are missing the truth.** We choose to struggle instead of embracing our power and advancing.

Once we individually and collectively realize what is happening, life for all of us will change dramatically. We will progress to a whole new level.

The turning point of this "***me***" extreme is an opportunity to advance the cause of life. If we fail to take advantage of the opportunity and forfeit our power, we die. And the lesson plays again for future generations.

We all succeed when we embrace and employ our power.

Employ your power. Accept responsibility. Live on purpose with faith. And yours will be a magnificent life.

PART 2

THE TRUTH ABOUT AMERICAN POLITICS

CHAPTER 9

CAN'T HANDLE THE TRUTH

I toyed with naming this section *A Master Course in Politics*. While "a master course" suggests exploring and defining the critical points of politics, *The Truth About American Politics* more accurately invokes a sense of the pervasive, dystopian nature of political misdirection, lies, and deceit dominating the American political scene these days.

In the United States and, unfortunately, too often around the world, politics is elevated to a lying, cheating, stealing art form, an art form with many accomplished masters. We are going to try to make sense of the political art form.

POWER POLITICS

Politics is fundamentally about power. And power is something we all aspire to have. At its most basic level politics is the complex of relations between people. A broader and more generalized definition of politics is the art or science concerned with governing.

From a personal perspective, politics is about acquiring, employing, and maintaining power or control over our own lives in relation to other people. This, unfortunately, is typically attempted by trying to gain control of or by controlling others. People's quest for and management of power is genuine, incredibly significant, and universal.

We cannot escape politics any more than we can escape breathing. We desire to control our own lives – to be in control – to control what we think and experience. And we mistakenly think gaining control of our own lives requires we control others. But we will get into all that.

In this section, *The Truth about American Politics*, we examine politics, not the follies of political actors, but rather underlying political motivations and strategies, and the results those motives and strategies produce for better or worse in our democratic republic.

Better or worse always depends on your perspective, where you sit relative to the power flow and dynamic. What politically is terrible policy for a nation or its people is often quite lucrative for a privileged few. If you are one of the select few, you will have a view diametrically opposed to the many as to the utility of those policies and political decisions.

And that, that is the mess, that is politics.

HUMAN RELATIONS

While politics is a component of all human relations – families, friendships, and within neighborhoods and communities – in this section, we focus on formal political settings: governments, corporations, and large organizations.

What applies in formal settings applies in informal personal relationships as well.

Here, we reveal the fundamentals of politics.

If you are an idealist like me, you will be disheartened by what you read in *The Truth About American Politics*. Politics and human nature can be brutal.

As a perennial optimist, however, I still see good. I see progress. I see opportunity and possibility. We have made it here despite the confluence of forces working against society's advance. And if we can get enough people to see the light, we can pull ourselves together and advance further. Time will tell.

MOTIVES

One of the most challenging assessments we must make concerning politics – acquiring, using, and maintaining power – is motive.

Why do I, or why does an individual, or why do individuals together apply power as they do?

Am I, is an individual, or are individuals together applying power for personal advantage?

Or am I, or are they or a group attempting to apply power for the advancement of others, for collective benefit, or for a greater good?

Discerning and distinguishing motives is no easy task.

As J.P. Morgan said: "A person always has two reasons for doing anything. A good reason, and ***the real reason***."

To understand politics, we examine the real reason: Why we do what we do.

TRUST

We are going to dig into and examine trust. All healthy and positive – that is non-destructively competitive – human relationships are built on a foundation of trust. Without trust, we cannot have functioning communities, a dynamic economy, or a viable open society. Without trust, we have conflict.

Trust is a foundational element of human power; therefore, trust is a foundational element of politics. We explore trust in some detail.

REALITY CHECK

From my perspective, the United States is in decline. I realize, however, that your position on advance or decline is relative to where you stand.

To illustrate how the United States is doing overall, I use the eighty-twenty rule. While reality is more nuanced than 80-20, 20 percent of Americans are doing great, while 80 percent are somewhere between treading water and sinking fast.

If you have been concerned about America's decline, you have probably wondered: Are Americans really that stupid? And are politicians really that inept, incompetent, or corrupt?

We continue to ruminate on these apparent enigmas as we proceed. The answers to those questions are not as simple as they seem.

LEADERSHIP

We will also explore the idea of leadership in further detail. Human society and the human experience are all about relationships. We are social beings. What other people think and do matters. What others do influences us, not all the time and everywhere, but often enough. Most of us go along to get along. And there are always outliers: people who are highly motivated and driven and those who are not motivated or driven. Most of us are in the middle – not driven, but not sloths either.

Like life is all about relationships, the advancement or decline of society is all about leadership – taking the right cues from the right people and moving in the right direction.

Many Americans look to politicians for leadership. Looking to politicians for leadership is like placing a rattlesnake on your front walkway to deter burglars. While it may be effective in the short term, it is generally not a good idea. Politicians have a purpose. But in a democratic society, that purpose must be carefully managed. Something we, the people, have been failing to do.

In the final chapter of this section, I point to the foundational revival changing course requires – the change we, the people, must make. In the *Epilogue*, I offer practical prescriptions for advancing together. We can only measure the efficiency and effectiveness of collective solutions in hindsight. We will not know what is possible unless and until we try.

As the African adage advises: "If you want to go fast, go alone. If you want to go far, go together." We can go far fast, but only if we go fast together.

Before we charge ahead, we must come to terms with the fundamentals.

What is the truth about politics?

CHAPTER 10

THE UGLY TRUTH

Plato once declared, "The price of apathy toward public affairs (politics) is to be ruled by evil men."

Sounds rather ominous. We will dissect the "evil men" part later (we addressed some of this in Part 1), but the "being ruled" part is something that concerns us all.

Plato softened his harsh, evil-men sentiment with another observation, "One of the penalties for refusing to participate in politics is that you end up being governed by your inferiors."

Napoleon Bonaparte furthered Plato's claim, determining, "In politics, stupidity is not a handicap." Something you are all too aware of if you have been keeping up with politics in America these last number of years.

Plato's highlighting of "inferiors governing" is not as ominous as evil men. However, still, it should cause us to consider we shouldn't leave this "governing thing" up to others, unsupervised. If we do not pay attention, do not play a part, or do not say something and do something, there is no telling where we could end up.

As Plato suggests, it may not be such a great place.

POLITICS DEFINED

We have already considered a definition of politics.

The word itself – politics – originates from the Greek politika, referring to the "affairs of the city," the city-states of ancient Greece. At a macro level, we define politics as activities associated with governance of a country or any other place. Governance is making decisions in groups or through forms of power relations, resolving conflicts among individuals or parties having or hoping to achieve power. Achieving power is attaining status, influence, or control over resources and people.

Said another way, politics comprises all the activities of cooperation, negotiation, and conflict within and between societies, whereby people organize, use, produce, or distribute human, natural, and other resources to sustain physical and social life.

Some think of politics as a distinctive form of rule whereby people act together through institutionalized procedures to resolve differences, reconcile diverse interests and values, and make public policies to pursue common purposes.

Or, as Ernest Benn once said (often attributed to Groucho Marx), "Politics is the art of looking for trouble, finding it whether it exists or not, diagnosing it incorrectly, and applying the wrong remedy."

On a micro level, politics is the use of power to determine who gets what, when, and how. Some, notably Vladimir Lenin, consider politics the most concentrated expression of economics. Others argue that at the root of all politics is conflict. One commentator notes *that politics is about the characteristic blend of conflict and cooperation found so often in human interactions. Pure conflict is war. Pure cooperation is true love. Politics is a mixture of both.*

As realists Machiavelli and Hobbes suggest – politics is the use of power, irrespective of the ends pursued, including the use of intrigue or strategy to obtain power in public or private spheres.

I now draw a distinction that oversimplifies, but please bear with me.

We can define extremes in virtually any aspect of life: hot–cold, light–dark, good–evil, and so on. For most of us, however, life happens not at extremes but in the gray area in between. We live life on the spectrum, the continuum somewhere between the extremes.

My distinction regarding politics: *The use of power employed for the benefit of a* ***few*** *or* ***many***. For the ***few*** or the ***many***. The fewest of the few is one. The greatest of the many is all.

Politics is fundamentally about seizing, wielding, and maintaining power. On a micro level, this is power an individual has over another. At a group level, it is power over others. And on a societal level, it is power over all.

The U.S. Declaration of Independence asserts: "We hold these truths to be self-evident, that all men are created equal, that they are endowed by their creator with certain unalienable rights, that among these are life, liberty and the pursuit of happiness."

While all people may be created equal and endowed with certain rights, not everyone has the same talents, abilities, and ambitions. All people have desires: to go places, to do things, to have things, and to control things. But not all people have the same desires, capacity, or act in the same way.

Human beings naturally and automatically compete for what they want – competing is nature's way. In healthy societies, competition translates into collaboration to benefit everyone. In unhealthy societies, competition manifests as conflict, with some individuals or groups attempting to dominate other individuals or groups. The conflict of competition ultimately results in the many – most of the people – serving a few.

POLITICS IS SIMPLE

The ugly truth is that **politics is a power game.**

The same principles of politics – competing for power – apply in democracies, oligarchies, or autocracies – whether the autocrats are dictators, monarchs, tribal chiefs, or corporate executives. The same political principles apply to governments, for–profit and not–for–profit corporations, educational institutions, states, provinces, counties, territories, municipalities, cities, towns, boroughs, communities, business establishments, neighborhoods, families, and personal relationships.

Wherever there are people, there is politics – the struggle for, use, and potential abuse of power. The fundamentals of the game are everywhere and always the same.

Check out ***The Dictator's Handbook*** by Bruce Mesquita and Alastair Smith for an eye-opening perspective on the game of politics. The subtitle of *The Dictator's Handbook* says it all: ***Why bad behavior is almost always good politics.***

Despite all we know about human society and the potential for us to achieve greatness collectively, the ugly truth about politics is that politics is often simply a competition for power. Rarely for all. Sometimes, for many. Usually, for a few.

Most commonly, politics becomes the struggle to gain, wield, and hold power for the benefit of a few.

Are you familiar with the book ***All We Really Need to Know We Learned in Kindergarten?***

Learning the proper lessons in kindergarten, we discover our strengths and weaknesses and the strengths and weaknesses of others. Then, we connect and collaborate to capitalize on those strengths and mitigate weaknesses. We learn to, and all advance together.

If we learn the wrong lessons in kindergarten, however, we compete. The best, most effective competitors seize power. The rest are vanquished or submit. Ultimately, we all suffer. We never reach our true potential. To achieve our true potential, everyone must contribute. Reaching our potential depends on the contributions of others. An oppressive power dynamic lessens the collectives' potential.

Politics – the obsession with power – often becomes the art and science of taking from the many to enrich the few.

Power corrupts, and absolute power corrupts absolutely. The nature of power is to corrupt.

So, let us consider nature once more...

CHAPTER 11

IT'S A JUNGLE OUT THERE

Thinking of the American governance model, we harken back to the ideas of *Enlightenment* thinkers, such as John Locke, Jean-Jacques Rousseau, and Adam Smith. *Enlightenment* thinkers influenced America's founding fathers: Benjamin Franklin, Thomas Jefferson, Alexander Hamilton, and James Madison, among others.

The ideas expressed in *Enlightenment* thought included individual rights and equality of all men. These were theories. Even though philosophically referring to humans and all men, equality and rights only applied to relatively wealthy, that is, relatively powerful, white male landowners. The philosophy was enticing and aspirational, but the reality differed.

Though never realized, the ideals of individual rights and equality are worth striving for. And those ideals make for exceptional marketing. So, with great pains, through violence, wars, and by way of much killing, America has moved toward those ideals. Yet still, we take one step forward and sometimes two steps back. Progress is rarely steady or consistent.

Plato, Aristotle, and others had mined many of the progressive ideas millennia before *Enlightenment* Europeans took them up. The ideas gathered momentum in the 17th and 18th centuries.

In addition to individual rights and equality, debating the character and nature of civil society led to the idea of basing legitimate political power on the consent of the governed.

Enlightenment thinking, while stressing what favored individuals – individual rights, equality, and consent – focused clearly on a cooperative, collaborative social contract by and between the body politic. *Enlightenment* thinkers realized individuals benefit most when the collective works harmoniously and cooperatively.

Taking some liberties with Adam Smith: *It is not from the benevolence of others we benefit, but rather from their regard for their own self-interest.*

Remember that distinction between extremes in the last chapter: light–dark, fast–slow, good–evil. Consider the extremes of ***I-me-my***, politics for the few versus politics for the many, ***we-us-together***.

Enlightenment thinkers realized as social beings, individuals benefit most when we, all of us, collectively work for our own benefit together. This sounds like a dichotomy, but it manifests our social nature. Adam Smith's invisible hand of accumulated self-interest results in a greater benefit for everyone. Conflict, at the extremes of competition, destroys. While mutual striving, on the other hand, builds. Working together, "value creators" add value and generate wealth for everyone's benefit.

Think of this contrast of the few, ***I-me-my*** versus the many, ***us-we-together*** as the potential of one person alone versus the potential of many people together. The potential of the many is far greater than an individual alone. Human society is greater than the sum of its parts. These insights, implemented in the American experiment in self-governance, painstakingly ushered in significant changes.

But did the changes last?

Were they changes that could last?

Did progressive changes conform with fundamental human nature?

IT'S A JUNGLE OUT THERE

You have probably, at times, thought of life as a struggle, a dog-eat-dog world. The law of the jungle says it is *survival of the fittest*; *kill or be killed*; *might makes right*. The biggest, baddest, strongest, fastest, and most cunning rule; and, as is the way of nature, should rule. Fundamentally, life is about survival.

As mentioned in *Part 1*, Charles Darwin is best known for his *Theory of Evolution*. Darwin refined the notion of natural selection to explain how living organisms compete to survive and reproduce. In simple terms, life always seeks to express more life. Life intends to grow and expand.

Darwin saw a process operating in nature, a random method of natural selection whereby offspring developed various traits. Some offspring adapted more effectively to their environments and competed better than others. Those that competed best were most likely to survive and reproduce, sharing traits with their offspring, allowing the next generation to compete more effectively. Over time and through many generations, individual organisms adapt to changing environments and compete more effectively.

Life intends to express more life. Life uses this process of natural selection, which plays out through direct competition.

Enough generalities. Let us bring this into the realm of the human social community. We consider the motives and intent of individuals in the next chapter; for now, let us focus on politics.

Niccolo Machiavelli, that Italian Renaissance diplomat, philosopher, and writer, sometimes called the father of modern political philosophy, is best known for ***The Prince***, written in 1513. Machiavelli did not consider political competition through a moral lens; he saw public and private morality differently. Machiavelli saw politics as a game, a competition. The objective of the political game is to win by seizing and holding power. In this game, the ends – seizing and holding power – always justify the means.

Machiavelli recognized the best political players – that is the successful ones – often use deception and treachery to win the game. Machiavelli advised that to rule well, a ruler must be willing to act unscrupulously at the correct times. It is better to be widely feared than to be greatly loved. Even in the face of moral corruption – looking out for a few at the expense of many – the social benefits of stability and security can be achieved.

It sounds like the jungle, like survival of the fittest for those playing the power politics game.

Thomas Hobbes, an English philosopher mentioned earlier, is also considered a founder of modern political philosophy. Hobbes followed Machiavelli by a century or so. Hobbes's masterwork ***Leviathan***, published in 1651, was a formulation for a functioning society after the agonizing struggle of the English Civil War. Hobbes declared the state a monster, created under the pressure of human needs, ultimately dissolving from the strife of human passions. Hobbes advocated for a unifying sovereign – a king – to protect society.

Left to their own devices, in other words, governing themselves, Hobbes saw humans as overly susceptible to passions and manipulation. People need a guiding light and a strong hand to maintain social order and discipline. Society devolves into chaos without a master wielding a firm rein to maintain order. The unconstrained competition in the jungle results in everyone competing with everyone for everything, all the time, everywhere. As Hobbes put it, '...the breakdown of the political community, [results in] continual fear, and danger of violent death; ... [in the natural state of humankind] the life of man [is] solitary, poor, nasty, brutish, and short."

As mentioned in *Part 1*, in the 19th century, After Darwin's theory of evolution grew in popularity, other theorists, such as Herbert Spencer, began floating notions soon labeled *Social Darwinism*.

Social Darwinism suggests whoever wins should win as it is the order of nature. Whoever seizes power should have power, as through natural selection, that is the way it is meant to be. The potentially violent establishment of a hierarchy is the social order. In other words, those with the power rightly deserve the power.

Social Darwinism was and is a theory used to justify all measure of immoral behavior perpetrated by the powerful on the powerless. *Social Darwinism* says whoever has the power rightly has the power. But if you take the theory from its grounding, whoever seizes the power rightly has the power. This is a self-reinforcing argument for endless conflict.

Social Darwinism's justification: "That's how things are meant to be" is a rather sobering and desperate argument.

Can this be so?

Are we animals?

CHAPTER 12

PEOPLE POWER

Humans are a paradox, a mystery wrapped in a riddle secured with a puzzle bow. Let us try to sort us out.

Society is a collection of individuals functioning more or less in harmony, frequently less. The potential of society is greater than the sum of its parts, but the parts matter.

Many people believe we human beings are just an advanced evolution of animals. Some argue we are not really an "advanced" evolution of animals, just another evolution of animals. A quick survey of the problems we cause around the globe validates this argument.

Through natural selection, we develop and express traits: attributes, talents, skills, and abilities; strengths and weaknesses; and we exhibit a measure of motivation or drive. The best we can hope for in the Darwinian model is to be blessed with the optimum traits and sufficient drive to survive and thrive.

If you adhere to this *humans-as-animals* perspective, then welcome to the jungle. Let the contest, the competition begin. It is you against the world, *every man for himself*. I hope you have the right traits to compete effectively. Alliances with others are conveniences to **temporarily** concentrate power to overwhelm, defeat, and vanquish foes. It is *survival of the fittest*. Everyone is out only to advance their survival interests. Life is a game of thrones.

However, other thoughtful, observant individuals believe we humans occupy a unique position in the metaphysical expanse. Something more is afoot, something more than meets the eye or conforms to our physical senses in a single dimension of time and space. These people point to another dimension beyond the physical reality we see, hear, touch, taste, and smell. To something bigger. Something we might label as spiritual, outside of time and space.

From this spiritual perspective, individuals are not limited by specific traits – we can select, focus on, develop, and reinforce whatever attributes and talents we care to. And we rely on others who do the same – develop select advantageous traits. Our potential is virtually unlimited.

I have been referring to human beings as individuals and society as a collection of individuals: the few, ***I-me-my*** versus the many, ***us-we-together***. This distinction may not be accurate. What if individuals are simply part of a whole, like cells are parts of a body? In this case, what is best for individuals is what is best for the whole.

By my cursory observation, a preponderance of the evidence suggests we, human beings, first and foremost, look out for number one. It is ***I-me-my***, my survival, and my ultimate success that matter. Is this perspective limited?

Could we be first and foremost social beings with an ***other focus***? After all, many people have sacrificed and are sacrificing all they have, including their very lives, so those they care about might survive and flourish.

Imagine that. Quite a thought.

Isn't that what love is?

Is love, this other focus – putting someone else's interests before our own – part of our nature, or is it something we learn together?

If you believe something else is afoot and perhaps give credence to a spiritual dimension or a collective greater than ***I-me-my***, then life and politics – the power game – are something else entirely.

BACK TO BASICS

What motivates us to act?

We have needs and wants that we satisfy and express through traits, attributes, talents, skills, and abilities in an environment. Needs are must-haves. Wants are nice to have. Needs and wants arise through three levels of motivation: instinct, emotion, and intellect.

The base level of motivation is **instinct**.

We are semi-autonomous beings intent on expressing life by surviving and reproducing. Instincts motivate us to cry out as babies when hungry and need comfort. Instinct moves us to seek warmth and shelter and prompts us to find mates, nurture, and raise young. Instinct causes us to congregate in groups for safety and security. We, naturally and instinctively, are social beings.

Two of our most potent instincts, however, are governors. These instincts limit us: **fear** and the **need to conserve energy**.

Fear constrains us. For the most part, fear keeps us from acting rashly and from doing dumb things. Fear is a pervasive and powerful force in the human drama. The need to conserve energy is a practical adaptation to limited resources. Since food and other resources are not always abundantly available, we conserve what we have to see ourselves through. Fear and the need to conserve energy are two primary drivers influencing us as we engage in the adventure of life.

The second level of human motivation or driver of action is **emotion**. Emotion is the energy we feel within our bodies resulting from our interpretation of what we experience. How we interpret what we experience is very much under our control. **Determining what we think and how we feel is a human being's preeminent power.**

Since feeling is a component of the human experience, if presented with the option to feel better or worse, we always seek to feel better. We prefer pleasure over pain. People, from moment to moment, seek to feel better.

We ultimately convert experience – our interpretations of events and circumstances – into feeling, into emotions: good, bad, or indifferent. The energy of those emotions moves us to act. The energy manifesting as emotion causes us to select an option, a course of action which, we hope, points us ultimately toward better feelings. Since we always seek to "feel better," emotion motivates us to act. **We choose, decide, or select, and act based primarily on emotion.**

Emotions and instincts are human beings' primary motivators.

The third level of motivation is a unique capability: **intellect** – the **ability to think**.

While instinct and emotion are the primary drivers of human action, **intellect is our most distinctive and powerful tool for expressing life**. Intellect – our ability to think – allows us to see, choose, and act differently. Through deliberate thought, we can override instinct and emotion. Through intellect, we possess the ability to control our lives. Thought frees us from the confines of time and space. We have more options and other choices because of our ability to think, reason, and imagine. We need not be victims of circumstance.

Our ability to **think** is our most powerful asset to navigate life. Thought bridges the physical reality of time, space, and circumstance and the infinite dimension of spirit. Unfortunately, thinking requires energy and effort. **Thinking is at odds with our instinct to conserve energy.** So, in practice, most of us avoid thinking. We make decisions and act most commonly and usually by instinct or emotion. We typically only think to rationalize why we do what we do after the fact. And that – not thinking – is a good part of our political problem.

IT'S ABOUT THE FUNDAMENTALS

As we examine politics – how people gain and use social power – we must keep in mind the fundamentals of nature and the fundamentals of human nature.

Each of us comes into this world with enormous potential. We develop traits. Instinct, emotion, and intellect drive us. We can access and leverage the support and resources of others and the community. Life seems stacked in our favor.

So, how do we go so wrong?

Why are hundreds of thousands of people living on the streets in the United States when millions have multiple homes?

Why are children going hungry in a country with more than enough food?

Why are millions the world over dying of diseases we know how to cure?

These questions demand political answers. It is not about resources or know-how or knowledge. So many are struggling because of our use, misuse, and abuse of power.

People possess the power. We have what we need.

Why aren't we using what we have?

Why aren't we using our power well?

CHAPTER 13

WHY POLITICIANS ARE SO INEPT

When society is flourishing, progress outpaces problems. When society is failing, problems outpace progress.

Where would you say we are right now?

Are we growing, thriving, advancing? Or are we declining?

By most objective measures, American society is declining. Most people in America, eighty percent or so, are treading water or are sinking – from an economic, health, social, and ultimately spiritual perspective.

Look at our debt: government, corporate and personal. Look at the increasing rates of poverty, drug abuse, and crime. Look at our declining life expectancy. Even more ominously, as this is likely the underlying contributing factor to all facets of our decline, look at the deliberate and systematic undermining of truth resulting in the erosion of trust. You would have difficulty convincing me America is heading in a positive direction.

A small segment of the population, however, twenty percent or so, are doing magnificently well. For the few, things are going great. For the many, not so much.

Whose fault is that?

Why are a few succeeding brilliantly while most are struggling or failing miserably?

Are Americans really this stupid? Do we lack the mental capacity?

Are most just not willing to work hard?

Are politicians really that inept, incompetent, and corrupt?

Or is it all just politics?

It is not the capacity of human beings or society at large that is the problem. We possess the power, aptitude, and means to change, fix, and make things better for everyone. We choose not to. Which leads to the million-dollar question: **Why?** Why are we deliberately moving in the wrong direction?

POLITICS

Politics, though it does not have to be, is fundamentally an animal struggle – competition in the jungle, *survival of the fittest*; *kill or be killed*; *might makes right*. Politics is an animal struggle playing out in the human social arena.

We are all competing to survive. We are all competing to express more life and to thrive. We want to feel good. We want to make the most of this opportunity. Each of us has an unlimited wellspring of desires. We want to have more, do more, and become more. We believe we need more power to do all we aspire to do and achieve all we aspire to achieve.

As the human population expands, we increase our collective potential. We add more talent, skills, abilities, and capability. We increase society's potential. But we also add more competition, more people competing for resources and attention, more people competing against us.

We have two choices. I state these as a dichotomy, an either-or, when in truth, as I have expressed before, life happens on a continuum between extremes. Our two choices:

We can either:

Connect, cooperate, and collaborate to increase the pie, add value, and create more so everyone benefits—the ***we-us-together*** option.

Or…

We can compete to secure our piece of the pie, our piece of what already is—the ***I-me-my*** option.

My wife's grandfather, who we called *Grandfather*, used to say, with a smile on his face and a twinkle in his eye whenever food was around, "He who gets the most, eats the most." We are always competing.

Competing or collaborating is the enduring question driving the human social order and politics.

THE GAME WE PLAY

Throughout human history, the power struggle, the game of politics, has usually been waged violently with weapons. Carl von Clausewitz, a Prussian general and military theorist, famously described war as the continuation of politics with other means. If it is a jungle out there and it's *kill-or-be-killed* – then we better get to killing if we care to survive.

These days, in what we consider a more civilized age, the power struggle is most frequently waged with words. But winning the game, seizing, and holding power is so important, so valuable, and so prized that if words fail, those playing the game of politics will not hesitate to use the threat of physical force and violence or employ physical force and violence, if necessary, to achieve their objective.

From an amoral or animal perspective, we usually choose an option – compete or collaborate – after calculating each course of action's relative advantages and disadvantages. Determining a strategy, playing the game with words, or playing the game with weapons, comes down to that measure of calculus. Each side calculates its comparative power, relative positional advantage or lack thereof, and overall potential for victory.

Perceiving an advantage, we are likely to compete. If at a relative disadvantage, we seek an appeasing, cooperative, or collaborative course of action, outcome, or resolution.

If we have an absolute advantage – we are in a commanding power position – we demand or take what we want. In the jungle, when we have the might, we are right. Whoever has the power makes the rules and rules.

If in a position of absolute disadvantage, we succumb. We submit and attempt to survive.

WHAT EXACTLY IS POWER?

Power is control, authority, or influence over others.

In the jungle, size, strength, speed, and cunning give people power. In twenty-first century society, additional factors determine power: number of people, how motivated and united toward a common purpose those people are, and any intellectual, resource, or technical advantage those people command.

It is helpful to simplify and combine these factors into a single, relatively pervasive concept: How much money do they have?

While not weapons, resources, and know-how, money is the universal, standard, aggregating measure of wealth.

Wealth is anything we value. It can be property, physical resources, capital equipment, human social capital, knowledge, skills and abilities, creative capacity, motivation, and perceived value. Everything of value can be quantified and aggregated as money. In the United States, in "dollar" terms.

Money always and only represents potential control of people; the potential control of or employment of people doing something, the explicit and direct use of human beings' time, energy, and talent.

In this way, **wealth is only and always the aggregate of people's time; time, energy, and talent applied to determined ends.** Therefore, **political power, all social power**

we seek, is control over other people. The more people we control, the wealthier we are.

Politics is the game to decide who controls who and for what ends.

In the game of politics, survival is paramount, an absolute, but survival with the most significant amount of power possible is the preferred objective. *Power, power everywhere – but I prefer that power in* ***my*** *hands.*

Those who think American politicians are extremely stupid, ignorant, incompetent, inept, and corrupt fundamentally misunderstand the game politicians are playing. Politicians know what they are doing.

While politicians consistently appear incapable of doing the simplest things: math, science, communicating honestly, behaving morally, and so on, and they seem entirely incapable of seeing the obvious consequences of their actions, they are doing what they have been hired to do.

It is not about making America great again. It is not about forming a more perfect union, ensuring domestic tranquility, providing for the common defense, promoting the general welfare, and securing the blessings of liberty to ourselves and our posterity. Politics is about seizing, wielding, and maintaining power.

CHAPTER 14

POLITICAL LEADERSHIP, AN OXYMORON

*W*e employ power two ways: personal power controls self and political power attempts to control others.

Personal power is the closest to **equal** human beings get. We are born with potential personal power – the power to move, choose, and **think**. We can determine what we do, where we go, and how we respond to what we experience. Personal power is our outright power.

We are not born fully empowered, though. Many societies do not promote or relish the idea of people assuming personal power. Most of the world's population lives in restrictive societies where personal power is strictly constrained. In societies that do promote personal power – those freer societies – people grow and mature into their power.

This maturing happens in families. Parents assume nearly universal power over babies. The power dynamic shifts as children grow. In healthy families, children mature into their power.

Personal power, however, comes with a burden. **Along with personal power comes personal responsibility.** Accepting personal power to act means accepting personal responsibility for outcomes. You cannot have one without the other. Personal power always comes with personal responsibility. Power and responsibility are two sides of the same coin.

In more free societies, as awareness of a person's potential personal power grows, so does their understanding of personal responsibility. People then face a choice. They can both assume their power and accept that they are responsible for their own lives, or they can reject personal power and the responsibility that comes along with it and give up, forfeit, or give away their power.

We are social beings. The potential of the collective is undoubtedly far greater than the potential of an individual. People may be willing to direct their power or even give up personal power to achieve mutually beneficial ends – the collective self-interest Adam Smith referred to. Leadership is the art of inspiring people to use their power to achieve some collective, ultimately beneficial ends. Leadership is leading others for their own benefit.

Politics is assembling, collecting, or concentrating personal power, but not necessarily, and if we are honest, only sometimes for the benefit of those contributing their power. Men and women playing the political game rarely use genuine leadership. Instead, people playing power politics use carrots and sticks more frequently to aggregate and concentrate power.

Even better than carrots and sticks – handing out rewards and doling out punishments – more cost-effective tactics to leverage against unsuspecting and easily manipulated masses are dishonesty, deception, and deceit. These are the least costly and most influential political tools. Dishonesty, deception, and deceit are the political tools of choice today.

POLITICIANS ARE NOT LEADERS

Politicians are hired to seize, wield, and maintain power. The guise and charade of political leadership is to lie, cheat, steal, coerce, strong-arm, bribe, buy off, pay off, threaten, extort, and do whatever it takes to acquire power. None of this is leadership.

Remember our dichotomy? On the one hand, are the few, the ***I-me-my*** types competing in the jungle; on the other are the many, the ***us-we-together*** attempting to connect, cooperate, collaborate, and create. Leadership brings the many together. Politics most often is manipulating the many to benefit a few. Politicians achieve their objective not by uniting for mutually beneficial ends but by dividing and conquering.

Political leadership is an oxymoron. Politicians are not leaders looking out for the good of those they lead. Politicians play a power game.

We cannot be too quick to dismiss politicians as evil and corrupt. They are playing the game. They are competing in the jungle. In the jungle, there are no rules. Politicians are hired to play the political game by those looking to control others.

Politicians are not hired and installed to do anything for the greater good.

Operating under the quasi-restraints of a representative democracy, American politicians are world-class. They are not necessarily ignorant, uninformed, woefully detached from reality, evil, or corrupt. Politicians are doing precisely what they are supposed to be doing, what they have been hired to do: take from the many to enrich the few. Politicians take power from the people to empower their patrons. And they enrich themselves along the way.

BAD BEHAVIOR IS ALMOST ALWAYS GOOD POLITICS

In ***The Dictator's Handbook***, Mesquita and Smith explain all political power arrangements work the same way, whether in nation-states, corporations, or communities.

We all think we are right. We all think we know what is best. We are all a little selfish. We all vie for power. We all play the power game. Adept players, those willing to do whatever it takes, over time extract power from the many, those less willing to do whatever it takes, and concentrate that power with the few. Someone always wins the game – the game of politics. While society always loses.

Mesquita and Smith developed a model to illustrate this power dynamic at work – the political means of acquiring, employing, and holding onto power.

Three levels impact the flow of social energy: power. On the lowest level are the masses, which Mesquita and Smith call ***interchangeables***. *Interchangeables* represent the minimum necessary popular support required to maintain power. In a representative democracy such as the United States, these are the voters needed to achieve a plurality or majority in some cases. Typically, this is a relatively small portion of the population. At the national level, it usually takes twenty to twenty-five percent of the population to install a president.

At the next level of the power dynamic are what Mesquita and Smith label ***influentials***. These are the men and women who influence that minimum necessary popular support. *Influentials* are community leaders, labor leaders, pundits, celebrities, politicians, etc.

At the top of the political power dynamic are ***essentials***. *Essentials* are that coalition of powerbrokers who consolidate power and maintain the system. *Essentials* are the powerful few who benefit at the expense of the powerless many. *Essentials* are the wealthy – the men and women who control the most people.

Gaining and maintaining political power – control over people – is a matter of managing the three levels of the power dynamic.

Now, most of us, and I am speaking for myself here too, most of us like to think, "I'm not like that. I would **not** use power to benefit a few. If I had power, I would **not** lord it over many." That person is the rare exception. Personal power is ultimately empowering. But once separated from an individual

– once an individual gives up their power – that power is corrosive. Bearing the weight of another's or many others' power is a burden. Power corrupts, and absolute power – absolute control over other people – corrupts absolutely.

I will illustrate with a simple, seemingly harmless example.

Researchers staged a straightforward competition. Two individuals playing the board game *Monopoly*. One of the two randomly selected individuals was given an advantage. The person awarded the advantage began play with twice as much money as the other competitor. In addition, every time that "advantaged" person passed "*Go*," they received twice as much cash as their disadvantaged opponent.

While playing, the person with the advantage typically became showy and confident; you might say: cocky. The advantaged person often grew arrogant. After winning the game, the person with the advantage rarely even acknowledged that the advantage contributed to their victory.

So, it is with people in power. Those who have power, whether gained or given, begin to believe they are better than those with less power. The powerful believe, no matter how they came into power, that they are more deserving of power than the powerless. Ever heard of *the divine right of kings*? This innate psychological dynamic eventually evolves to *absolute authority* – absolute power.

This is the corrosive nature of power.

CHAPTER 15

ZOMBIE APOCALYPSE

Politics, the game of acquiring, using, and holding power, conforms to *the law of the jungle.*

The political game is played by carefully managing people who matter across three levels of the power dynamic: the ***interchangeables***, voters; the ***influentials***, those manipulating voters; and the ***essentials***, the real power players – the men and women who benefit the most by consolidating and wielding power.

Essentials unite to guarantee private rewards – power – flows their way. The *essentials* remain loyal to the political system and its leaders unless and until the power and benefits stop flowing. *Essentials* manage *influencers* through a combination of public and private rewards, ensuring the *influencers* do whatever is necessary to get the minimum support from the masses, the *interchangeables*, to retain power.

To optimize the power flow – to concentrate power in the power player's hands – the perfect political play is to never over-compensate or under-compensate the supporting cast. In politics, the greater good is never, ever a consideration. Politics is a fear-based, *survival* game.

AMERICAN POLITICS

Now that we have laid the foundation, let us examine American politics.

You may be familiar with the business adage: *Marketing getting out ahead of production*. That is, marketing often makes promises the product can never deliver. The United States of America has brilliant, universally appealing marketing. Look at our founding documents: *The Declaration of Independence* and the *Constitution*. Liberty, equality, justice, civil rights, property rights, the rule of law, the pursuit of happiness, and personal power. Opportunity. What's not to love? This is inspired and inspiring marketing.

The product, however – American democracy, the land of opportunity – even after 245 years, is still under development. The United States has both a breathtaking and deeply troubling political history.

The American political system has never come close to living up to its marketing. But the United States has more fully empowered people than any political system.

The first eighty years of the American drama were a matter of surviving while coming to terms with slavery. After the Civil War, over the next eighty years, and still not ending oppression, the adolescent nation came of age and assumed power on the world stage. To get to that commanding position, to get through the foibles of the 1920s, the Depression, and the Second World War, the masses gave up much of their power. Out of what the people perceived as a necessity, Americans came together, ceded personal power to political authorities – the government – and hoped for the best. Americans ultimately had to fight a world war to change the nation's trajectory.

Trust has methodically eroded over the last seventy-five years after the rebirth of freedom and the redistribution of power resulting from the Second World War. Power players have once again managed the power dynamic brilliantly. As power continues to concentrate and wealth and power steadily flow from the many to the few, the United States has resumed a downward trajectory.

Power corrupts. The American decline is the result of the corrupting nature of power.

PARTISAN COMPETITION

George Washington warned against political parties. He advocated citizens weigh ideas on merit and that those notions that expanded and promoted freedom and democracy and empowered people be adopted (for his version of the people – he was a slaveholder, after all). But other ambitious people had their own ideas. We all think we know best. The game was on.

Two political parties formed immediately in the United States – two opposing forces. Evolving over the years, we now have the Democratic and the Republican parties. The parties do their own marketing to influence that often elusive minimum number of required voters – the *interchangeables*.

The Democratic Party markets economic strength, affordable health care, justice for all, unity, diversity, world-class education, and American leadership.

The Republican Party markets a growing economy, limited government, strong military, secure borders, energy independence, and traditional values.

Both parties attempt to appeal to voters' instincts and emotions. But remember, party leadership is much less concerned about delivering a product – those promises – than they are about influencing voters – marketing. Party leaders of both parties are worried about winning a political game. The objective of the political game is seizing, wielding, and holding power, not delivering the goods of sound governance. Public messaging and marketing are very different from the ultimate private objective.

The revelation regarding the two major political parties is exposed not through what they market or say – it is demonstrated by what they do. Both parties use power to actively extract resources from the many and direct those resources to their power-player patrons – the few, the *essentials*.

The parties are akin to two competing product brands appealing to different market segments. But their objectives are the same. Take from the many to enrich the few. Watch where the money and, therefore, the power flows.

GROWING DISSATISFACTION

As wealth and power are extracted from the many, over time, the many – everyday, ordinary citizens – begin to realize their loss. Dissatisfaction and distrust of government, institutions of power, and each other grows among the masses. People become increasingly weary of the expanding wealth gap and its enlarged power gap and resent it. The *essentials*, always ready to exploit an opportunity, leverage the ever-increasing malaise and stoke further anxiety to advantage themselves.

Nearly eight of every ten Americans are trying to hold onto or are losing ground economically. Politicians – *influentials* working for political parties – continually promise they have the solutions to make things better for the people. But time and time again, what politicians deliver is more of the same: take from productive people and give to the privileged few. Frustration grows. But there is always a tipping point. A fixed game undermines motivation. Eventually, there will be nothing more to extract from the productive segment of society. Finally, calculating they have nothing to lose, the masses revolt.

FUELING THE FIRE

People do not like to think. For most, thinking is a last resort activity. Instead of using their intellects and verifying facts, people rely on ingrained bias and emotion to make decisions. So clever political operatives leverage prejudice and emotion to influence and manipulate the easily manipulated.

As the masses become more and more disenfranchised and seemingly helpless within a rigged system, they become more irritated, volatile, and dangerous. Politicians who appeal to bias and encourage explosive emotions are playing with fire.

Donald Trump stepping into the national political arena in 2014 was like dumping accelerant on a fire.

Born to a wealthy family, Trump came to believe he deserved power. Trump learned early the tried-and-true tactics of the political game and the utility of bullying. Working for his wealthy father, Trump realized that if people believe you have money, whether you do or not, you have power. Perception is power. He cleverly cultivated the perception of wealth even through his myriad bankruptcies. This always afforded him a position of power amongst those who did not know better.

An unabashed narcissist, always seeking personal validation, Trump recognized growing discontent amongst the masses. He stoked fear and hate, blaming everyone he could think of for what ails he could manufacture. Trump blamed immigrants, minorities, women, foreigners, the media, political opponents, anyone his audience was open to vilifying. He energized people's base instincts and emotions of fear and hate. Millions rallied to Trump's siren call.

Power brokers controlling the Republican Party initially resisted Trump's unconstrained onslaught on truth. After all, lying and cheating to steal had been carefully managed **covert** political tactics. Republican Party leadership quickly recognized, however, the utility of fear and hate Trump so crudely encouraged.

For the hapless masses, no need to think. And no need to assume personal responsibility. The truth is, 'whatever the powerful say it is,' and we are all competing anyway. The ends justify the means. Politicians stepped up their marketing, proclaiming: 'Problems are someone else's fault; those people you've always harbored a bias against. Direct your hate and anger toward them and give your power to me.'

An ageless tactic worked brilliantly and proved useful once again. We, the people, refuse to learn.

This, out in the open dissolving of truth and undermining of trust was the power players' perfect storm. The Republican Party closed ranks, funneling trillions of dollars from the many to the few unleashing the zombie apocalypse. It was like a virus – and not the coronavirus. Some unseen, highly-contagious pathogen infected millions. The infected masses were rendered unable to think while simultaneously enraged.

Americans ransacked the United States capital.

The acolytes of power are now openly promoting lying and cheating tactics to achieve the objective of stealing – taking from the many to enrich the few. Many still refuse to see the ruse – politics at its best. And millions of Americans are loving the game.

The game is ultimately about power, concentrating power. As Machiavelli said, the ends justify the means. Many are playing, but only a few appear to be winning. The truth is we all lose.

Are Americans really this stupid? What now?

CHAPTER 16 NOW WHAT?

CHAPTER 16

NOW WHAT?

Plato once observed, "Whatever deceives men seems to produce a magical enchantment." America is undoubtedly enchanted as we are terribly deceived through our politics. We dare not **think**, for if we did, we would discover the truth about American politics.

Concentrating power always results in disaster. Power corrupts, and absolute power corrupts absolutely.

A positive spin to this destructive nature of corrupting power is attributing the "creative destruction" the process inevitably invokes to the ways of nature. We can contentedly determine that power's corrupting influence is beyond our control. Society swings to an extreme concentrating power, resulting in catastrophic ruin. Then, society begins again. Hopefully, a phoenix will spring forth from the ashes.

Politics ultimately determines the economic and social fortunes of nations and peoples. Empowering the many is a path to economic and social prosperity. Disempowering the many or empowering a few at the expense of many, the usual, most common political path – the game of politics – is a recipe for conflict, violence, and destruction.

WE'RE AFRAID

Many see the jungles of time and space as dangerous. Believing ourselves alone in the jungle, we must determine: Is it every man for himself, me competing to survive? Or is it ***us-we-together*** endeavoring to thrive?

In the jungles of time and space, each one of us has the potential to claim an incredible gift: **personal power**. Personal power is the ability to interpret what we experience and determine where we go and who we become. **We can think and choose. Along with personal power, however, comes responsibility.**

Overwhelmed and intimidated by the jungle, rather than accept responsibility, most succumb to fear and seek an easier path. People forfeit their power and give it to others. And so the misfortune begins.

Even a system designed to distribute power, like the political system of the United States, will, given enough trials and time for the cunning to work their magic, devolve to concentrate power. As water seeks its own level, power flows to those willing to seize and use it.

Politics is the game of seizing, wielding, and maintaining power – control over people. In the jungle, there are no rules. Surviving justifies whatever means are necessary.

AN ATTEMPT

The founding fathers attempted to form a government to achieve two primary ends: expanding economic opportunity and ensuring national sovereignty. The confederacy of states proved unworkable, so the founders tried again. *The Constitution of the United States* defined a federal republic, a representative democracy comprised of three co-equal branches of government.

Promoting universally appealing, aspirational, and inspiring ideals but still accommodating the abomination of slavery, the *Constitution* allotted the federal government the centralized powers necessary to stimulate economic prosperity and ensure national security. The *Constitution* allocated to the states the powers to maintain social order and empowered the people like no people had ever been empowered before. The young nation grew and prospered.

The United States of America was a ground-breaking attempt at self-government – a bold experiment. But without deliberately managing the power dynamic and carefully redistributing power to continue progress, nature intervened taking its course through ebbs and flows and myriad trials and tragedies. Men and women burdened by personal responsibility and facing political dangers abdicated personal power. Those willing to compete concentrated that political power. Over time, the many came to serve the few.

WHEN YOU HAVE IT, KEEP IT

Only some rich and powerful achieve their status by employing Machiavellian political tactics. But all wealthy and powerful people acquire their power within a system promoting the concentrating of power. Systems constantly evolve to concentrate power.

Whenever you hear the rich and powerful condemn the poor and powerless, remember: the wealthy and powerful believe they deserve that wealth and power. Their criticism is not based on moral grounds, despite what they may say. The rich and powerful condemn the poor and powerless's actions that threaten their power. It is not morality. It is power.

Having wealth and power, the powerful believe the powerless should remain as they are. When you are winning, there is no need to change tactics.

CAN THE AMERICAN EXPERIMENT SURVIVE?

The American experiment can survive if **the people choose to assume the burden of personal responsibility.**

Assuming the burden of personal responsibility, the people – us, you, and I – must be willing to and actively seek to grow – connect, cooperate, collaborate, and create. We must be willing to create and contribute together. The alternative is to fight over what already exists and compete for spoils.

Today, typically, fewer than half of Americans vote. Most Americans opt out of playing the political game for good reason. Many believe they cannot win. Others believe playing does not matter. Most are content to get on with their lives. And who can blame them?

Unfortunately, the nature of the game, the system we have set up, demands people give their power to those willing to wield it. Rather than compete, participate, and hold those *representatives* accountable, most adapt to whatever circumstances are thrust upon them and try to make the best of things.

Without a disciplined system to actively manage and redistribute power, the forces of nature concentrate power. Life is a power struggle, but it need not be a political power struggle. Life is a struggle between:

Recognizing and accepting personal power and the attendant responsibility – ***us-we-together***.

Or rejecting personal power and competing in the jungles of time and space for political power – control of others – ***I-me-my***.

How a society distributes control – through personal or political power – determines the destiny of that society.

The United States is declining because the people refuse to see what is happening, the ugly truth of politics. Instead of realizing success is up to us, we run from responsibility. We forfeit power. We give power to the bold so we do not have to be responsible. We can blame someone else when we pay the price.

Saving America from ruin requires rebuilding trust and redistributing power.

A functioning democracy requires moral, educated, and informed citizens. If we **become trustworthy** and trust each other, we can do anything. First, we must stop the fear-and-hate train. Then, we must rewrite the rules of the political game.

This means reshaping and redesigning the political system. No more career politicians who are easily bought and paid for by powerbrokers. We must design a system where **the people** are the *essentials*.

We must fundamentally reform our corporate economic system to redistribute power and reinforce personal responsibility. Powerbrokers hide behind corporate shields, pillaging and plundering anonymously at will. It is a system Americans have grown wearily accustomed to. We must remove that cloaking device allowing the few to steal from the many.

There is much more to do, but if we cannot accomplish these – refurbish our political and economic system – we will never rebuild trust, and the American experiment is dead in the water. **Democracy only works if we empower people.**

The United States of America was founded on ideals of freedom, justice, and opportunity: equal treatment under the rule of law. Those ideals mean nothing if everyone does not have a stake, does not have a common view of reality, and does not do their part. Trust is broken, resulting from political misdirection speeding the pervasive concentration of wealth and power. It is as simple and as complex as that.

And that is the truth about American politics.

EPILOGUE

Are Americans really this stupid?

We have squandered a magnificent opportunity. We never had it all right, not even close. But after World War II, we were on a roll. We were pulling together. We were taking on challenges, and we were dreaming big again. Then we began to drift away from ***we-us-together***, and to focus on ***I-me-my***. And the decline began.

The United States has gone from the greatest creditor nation in history to the largest debtor nation in sixty years. Norm Franz once wrote:

Gold is the money of kings.

Silver is the money of gentlemen.

Paper is the money of peasants.

Debt is the money of slaves.

We have chosen debt as our money. We, most Americans, have enslaved ourselves. And we keep piling on more debt as fast as we possibly can.

Americans are so busy fighting over scraps we are in the throes of committing suicide. A few are succeeding spectacularly – concentrating wealth and power – while the masses struggle to get by. On the face of it, it seems like monumental stupidity. Maybe we really are this stupid. But maybe the course of our journey is beyond our control. Nature ebbs and flows. Empires rise and fall. We may not have the ultimate say. Our task is to endure the tumult, learn what we must, and do our best.

People naturally move from a ***we-us-together*** orientation to an ***I-me-my*** orientation, and the competition begins. For the last sixty years, in families, communities, corporations, and governments, we have been playing a political game – a power game. And in so doing, we have been eroding trust – the foundation of society.

When people connect, collaborate, and create, communities prosper. Prosperity, however, sows the seeds of its undoing. Prosperity makes room for individuals to maneuver for status.

Nature says, "compete to survive." To survive, we must rely on one another. We must come together, connect, collaborate, and cooperate. When we do – when we come together, connect, collaborate, cooperate, and create – we thrive. But nature advances in cycles. Nature dictates the cycle of life: birth, growth, maturing, decline, death, decay – rebirth. The cycle works for individuals and the many together. Maybe the cycle is beyond us to affect. But maybe not.

Rather than leave our fate to the whims of chance, we can choose differently and generate better results. We can help a phoenix rise from the ashes. We get to decide what we think, where we go, what we do, and how we feel. We can change our course. When we do, we change our destination and our destiny.

Much is required to fix America – to get the United States on the right track. Progress hinges on the people – Americans. The enemy is not **THEM**, "People who do not look like us or sound like us or even think like us." **The enemy is within.** To rebuild trust we must open ourselves to grace. We can figure this out if we can trust each other enough to come together.

HOW?

First, we must get off the fear-and-hate-victim train. We must stop clinging to delusions feeding self-righteous hubris. We must finally realize that people who see things differently are not enemies.

A functioning democracy requires moral, educated, and informed citizens. America is falling short. We would rather not seek truth or deny uncomfortable truths than face and deal with reality. Too often, we seek and choose the easy wrong way over the hard right way.

Those who compete well choose to play the political power game and dominate. Those who do not compete well fail to see the truth. Lacking the courage and conviction to shoulder personal responsibility we refuse to embrace our power. Being unwilling to embrace personal responsibility, we are not worthy of trust. So, by our choices, the social network crumbles.

If we can become trustworthy, and if we can trust, we can do anything together. That anything begins with reclaiming our power. Reclaiming personal power reestablishes a myriad of opportunities. From a solid foundation, we can move forward again.

A few hire politicians to consolidate power for those few. American politicians do an extraordinary job. They have no interest in changing a system they are succeeding in, so I propose three foundational reforms:

1. A grass-roots leadership and educational effort to reorient Americans to the truth about power, freedom, and responsibility.
2. A constitutional convention to fundamentally reshape public service, redesign our election process, and eliminate our "pay to play" system. No more career politicians to be bought and paid for by corporate interests.
3. A fundamental redesign of our corporate system. Malfeasance abetted by legal but corrupt corporate practices allows the powerful to pillage and plunder anonymously at will. We must stop the few from stealing from the many.

Democracy only works if we empower the people.

Because of the corrosive nature of power, concentrating power undermines community and prosperity. The solution is not what we typically malign as "socialism" – absolving people of personal responsibility and the motivation of personal incentive. **The solution is to show people the potential of their personal power.**

The United States of America was founded on ideals of freedom, justice, opportunity, and equal treatment under the rule of law. Those ideals mean nothing if all the people do not have a stake, do not have a shared common view of reality, and do not do their part. Trust is broken due to political misdirection to concentrate wealth and power. The truth is as simple and complex as that.

Civility is a reasonable start. But America's politics and politicians are entrenched. Every administration and every congress continues to play musical chairs with disastrous results. If we are interested in saving these United States, Americans must do something **bold**, **now**. **We must change ourselves** and then purge the corruption. As tricky as personal responsibility may be, Americans can and will step up to the challenge.

Nations prosper when many share the burden and the benefits, yet the American system has evolved to enrich the few at the expense of the many. The cycle continues. We are at the low point of the cycle: the crisis and chaos phase. It is time for something radical. It is time for people to **think**, embrace honesty and integrity, and stop the charade of lies and deceit. Enough.

For America to survive this transition and be reborn, the people must be willing to **think**. We must muster the courage to bear responsibility and stop blaming the powerless. We cannot expect politicians to fix things. Politicians are playing the power game. Nothing will get fixed until Americans **revise the game and change the rules.** Of the people, by the people, for the people, it is up to the people to change. Saving America requires **we, the people, change**.

Extraordinary men have tried to guide us to overcome fear and hate before: Jesus Christ – executed; Abraham Lincoln – assassinated; Mahatma Gandhi – assassinated; Martin Luther King, Junior – assassinated. Overcoming fear and hate is not easy. No one is standing on the moral high ground to show Americans the way. It is up to the people to do the right thing together.

We must gather the courage to claim and use personal power, not for wealth and privilege like the elites, but for good. We must act together.

If we do not find the courage to connect and collaborate, to trust, to remake the fragile democracy, then it is not: *May God bless America.* It is:

May God have mercy on us all.

ACKNOWLEDGEMENTS

*E*verything I have done, everything I do, and everything I am yet to accomplish is made possible by the loving and supportive people who surround me and those who are drawn into my awareness. My success is made possible by divine inspiration and the genius and generosity of countless people.

I am forever grateful for Lisa, my wife, my two terrific children, Merideth and Mitchell, and all my family and friends. I am truly blessed to have wonderful people in my life.

I extend my most heartfelt thanks to past sages, modern-day prophets, and those searching diligently to express truth through insightful words and faithful examples. The courage, commitment, and sacrifice of men and women who embrace the opportunity that is life inspire me.

I pray that the words etched on these pages inspire you to take on laudable challenges, endure worthwhile hardships, and fulfill what I know to be limitless potential.

ABOUT THE AUTHOR

Scott F. Paradis, Change Agent, is a student of life and seeker of ultimate truth. Believing simplicity is the gateway to understanding; he's made it his mission to unearth and distill foundational truths, empowering people to unlock their full potential.

Attempting to lead by example, Scott encourages people to dream big, build faith, and relate to others and life in positive, rewarding ways by establishing life-affirming habits of thinking, feeling, and acting. Scott's personal aspiration is for his life to be a message of hope, an example of faith, and an expression of love as he works to make the most of himself by doing the best he can with what he's got.

A native of New Hampshire, Scott served more than three decades in the United States Army, rising to the rank of colonel. His military adventure included varied stateside assignments and tours in Europe and the Middle East. His intellect and insight led him to a prestigious *Congressional Fellowship* with the United States Senate and a transformative *National Security Fellowship* at Harvard University's John F. Kennedy School of Government.

Scott holds a Master of Science in Administration from Central Michigan University and a Bachelor of Arts in Sociology from the University of New Hampshire.

He and his wife, a shining star – the former Lisa Newcombe – live in Eagle River, Alaska. Scott explores the Alaska mountains at every opportunity with his hiking buddy – a 95-pound golden doodle, Rusty.

Contact Scott F. Paradis to schedule a presentation, workshop, or consult:

ScottFParadis.com

(703) 772-3521

Scott@c-achieve.com

https://www.linkedin.com/in/scott-f-paradis/

Available from *Scott F. Paradis*

CAPITOL CRIMES
Is That a Knife in Your Back?

ARE AMERICANS REALLY THIS STUPID?
Are Politicians Really This Inept?

SHEEP, HERDERS, WOLVES
Why We Are Where We Are: A Modern American Fable

EXPLOSIVE LEADERSHIP
The Ultimate Leader Training Experience

MONEY
The New Science of Making It

HIGH PERFORMANCE HEALTH AND FITNESS HABITS
Engage Your Health and Fitness Auto-Pilot

HIGH PERFORMANCE HABITS
Making Success a Habit

HOW TO SUCCEED AT ANYTHING
In 3 Simple Steps

SUCCESS 101 HOW LIFE WORKS
Know the Rules, Play to Win

WARRIORS DIPLOMATS HEROES
Why America's Army Succeeds
Lessons for Business and Life

PROMISE AND POTENTIAL
A Life of Wisdom, Courage, Strength, and Will

Look for these and other online audio and audio-visual programs by Scott F. Paradis:

https://ScottFParadis.com

EXPLOSIVE LEADERSHIP

The Ultimate Leader Training Experience

FOLLOW THE MONEY

It's Never About the Money

HIGH PERFORMANCE HEALTH AND FITNESS HABITS

Engage Your Health and Fitness Auto-Pilot

SUCCESS 101 HOW LIFE WORKS

Focus on Fundamentals

www.ingramcontent.com/pod-product-compliance
Lightning Source LLC
LaVergne TN
LVHW010923110826
845149LV00013B/2460